ANTS, VINES, AND CHURCHES

CHARLES SIMPSON

csm publishing

csm publishing

An imprint of
CHARLES SIMPSON MINISTRIES
P.O Box 850067
Mobile, AL 36685-0067 U.S.A.

For information about special discounts for bulk purchases,
please contact CSM Publishing at
customer.service@csmpublishing.org

For more information about Charles Simpson Ministries
and to order this book as well as other resources online, visit:
www.csmpublishing.org

Printed in the United States of America.

To those who love the Church

TABLE OF CONTENTS

Introduction 11

Chapter 1: My Journey...................................... 17

Chapter 2: The Changing Church..................... 31

Chapter 3: The Flow of Life.............................. 45

Chapter 4: Flowerpots and Vines..................... 57

Chapter 5: Army Ants....................................... 71

Chapter 6: Know Your Sphere.......................... 87

Chapter 7: Lead Your Sphere........................... 97

Chapter 8: Increasing Your Sphere................. 107

Chapter 9: The Cross and the Kingdom........... 117

Chapter 10: Connecting With Men................... 129

Chapter 11: The Flow of Money...................... 141

Chapter 12: The Mystery of Fellowship........... 153

INTRODUCTION

THE CHURCH IS ALIVE AND CHANGING. IT is more than an institution; it is the body of Christ, and living things change, adapt and reproduce. The purpose here is to seek understanding as to how the Church is changing, how it is adapting to a very different world, and how it can reproduce and multiply in that environment.

I was licensed to preach in 1955 by a Southern Baptist Congregation and have since birth been involved with Church life. My involvement has gone beyond being Southern Baptist, and I will discuss that in the first chapter. I have grown to respect many traditions while failing to be satisfied with traditions as a guide to the future.

I love the history of the Church, especially those dedicated people who were led by the Holy Spirit to press the Church toward its destiny. Their journey was dangerous, exciting, and greatly rewarding to those of us who enjoy their victories. But to entertain the notion that the Church has arrived is to disregard their passion for the purpose of God, and it is a denial of the Holy Spirit who is still speaking.

The Holy Spirit, our Guide, is leading us on a journey. History and the Bible both emphasize this truth. Jesus is the Author and Finisher of Our Faith, the Alpha and the Omega, the Beginning and the End. He is the Seed of Abraham, planted in the world to bring a Harvest among all Nations. The Church has always been sojourning toward its Divine purpose.

There are many questions for those of us who agree that we are on a journey: Where will it take us? How will we get there? What will the mature Church look like? What should we do now? And there are many questions within the boundaries of faith that are necessary. The disciples asked Jesus many questions; He was never threatened by them.

This book is not about the "end-time". It is about us and how we will respond to the great challenges of the Church. It is about adapting and reproducing in cultures that are hostile to our message. Many books have been written on these issues and will be. All of them can serve to provoke our thinking, and I pray that this one will too.

One author asked his friend, "Have you read my last book?" "I hope so," his friend replied. Well, I do not know if this will be my last book, but I'm sure there will be revisions as I see more clearly in the future. We know and prophesy in part. So this work is offered in humility, for good reason.

Since the Church consists of people, the focus will be on the kind of people that we produce. Those who measure the Church by quantity while ignoring the quality of the product will continue to be marginalized and disrespected by the culture that they hope to influence. If the corporate value is not firmly incarnated into individuals, no structural tampering will make us effective

Since Jesus is the Holy Seed of Church life, we will constantly look to Him in His Incarnation as the model for our quest. It is my opinion that Jesus is not only the Son of God, He is the Way, the Truth, and the Life and His ways are higher than ours. I do not believe that we have improved on His ways and how He produced disciples. We must not forget that Jesus was not only Divine; He was smart and wise.

To suggest that we can arrive at our destiny by methods alone, even His methods, would be a mistake. Malachi chapter 3 refers to those who fear the Lord as His "jewels." Jewels are not formed by methods but by a process of extreme heat and pressure. It takes tribulation to enter the Kingdom. So, we will discuss the relevance of the Cross to bringing those that fear the Lord to maturity. This will not be a market-driven approach.

The true seed will flourish even in adversity as it does now in many parts of the earth. The victory of the believer and the Church carries a heavy implication of testing. The winnowing process must not be overlooked in our quest for God's purpose.

The dross of personal preference will be burned away.

Much of the Western Church in Europe and North America is caught in the web of a secular culture and immobilized by intimidation. The Gospel is not politically correct, especially the message of our need to be saved from ourselves. An additional challenge is that the Church has slumbered through the challenge of rising Islamic militancy and reproduction. While westerners abort their young and seek personal security and consumption, Islam multiplies through childbirth and migrates into the West without assimilating into its culture.

Many great European church buildings are now little more than museums memorializing a once vibrant faith. Universities in Europe and America, founded by Christian scholars, are now fountains of secular militancy. And so, hostility to the Gospel of Jesus Christ is formidable.

Does all of this bode ill for the Church? No, but it bodes ill for passive attitudes and stale methods that ignore the warnings of Jesus and the apostles. The church that ignores its own complacent product and marginalized position in culture is already virtually irrelevant to the future.

What must we do to become the "light of the world?" For one thing, we must produce lights *in* the World. It is all in the person that we send out the door after the benediction. It is not what we get people into, it is what we get into them. Encouragement and inspiration without foundations, equipping, and purpose is like fueling a vehicle that has no engine.

So how can we fix the vehicle? If the vehicle is the individual believer instead of the corporate church, if it is the person and not the meeting, if it is personal structure and not only church structure, then we must shift our focus. This book is about that. It is about a refocus on the person that we produce, and their effectiveness in the world.

CHAPTER ONE
MY
JOURNEY

THIS IS NOT AN AUTOBIOGRAPHY, THOUGH it is autobiographical at some points. Personal history will provide a context for my view of the Church journey.

My dad and mom were Baptist Missionaries in the bayous of South Louisiana. Mom was from that area, raised in a Roman Catholic, French-speaking culture. In the 1930s, South Louisiana was remote with no electricity and much of its transportation was on the water. People were primarily farmers, trappers, and fishermen. Oil was just being discovered there.

This was a tough area for an evangelical minister. The culture was strongly attached to Catholicism, with large churches, convents, and monasteries in almost every village. A book could be written on the process evangelizing there, but that is not our purpose here. Dad did succeed in establishing several churches in those areas.

How Dad got involved in South Louisiana goes back to the Great Depression; economic difficulty caused him to drop out of college in Birmingham, Alabama, and go to New Orleans to work for a trucking company. He continued his education at New Orleans Baptist Theological Seminary and attended a local Baptist church. The pastor of that church had a strong desire to reach into the bayous. Dad got involved.

> **Dad pitched a large tent on the levee of the Mississippi River and approximately 1,500 people attended revival meetings. This was amazing because the population was sparse; people came from miles around.**

The difficulty of the task drove those who were engaged in trying to evangelize there to seek the Holy Spirit's help. In the process they were baptized in the Holy Spirit and received gifts of the Holy Spirit. They prayed each night for eight months. That was in 1931 and 1932.

The team began to have success. Dad pitched a large tent on the levee of the Mississippi River near Port Sulphur, south of New Orleans, and approximately 1,500 people attended revival meetings. This was amazing because the population was sparse; people came to the meetings from miles around.

One of those who came was from a remote village on Grand Bayou—a village of mixed race with no law. The man who came was the town's "strong man." He met Christ and his village followed him; a church was built. There are other stories, but this snapshot will give some background.

Mom was part of a house group consisting mainly of her family and relatives–Germans who had settled among the French and spoke French. She was one of twelve children. She and most of her family were baptized in a muddy bayou one December day. Dad and Mom married in 1935.

The "Pentecostal" elements had faded from Dad's ministry prior to his marriage, because of controversy and theological issues. He and the others avoided the Pentecostal identity and remained Baptist, but there was controversy. The issues were "eternal security," "sinless perfection," women pastors, and what they deemed as emotionalism. It would be 40 years later before he would tell me the whole story.

I was born in 1937, in New Orleans Baptist Hospital, but my parents were now living deep in bayou country near my mother's family. One of my earliest memories was the home-made house trailer in which we lived. Not far away—"a rock's throw"—was the swamp with its gators and wildlife. Nearby

> **I remember the home meetings too, lying on a pallet with other children while the older folks sang and prayed and then Dad would teach. Sometimes, I could see the chickens under the house through the cracks in the floor.**

was Grandpa's syrup mill, where he ground sugar cane and cooked the juice. The road that passed our trailer was made of oyster shells and gravel; you could hear the occasional truck or car that passed a long way off. There were few sounds, mostly those of birds and animals.

I remember the home meetings too, lying on a pallet with other children while the older folks sang and prayed and then Dad would teach. Sometimes, I could see the chickens under the house through the cracks in the floor.

We moved from there to Golden Meadow, a village along the Bayou La Fourche. La Fourche was a 90 mile long bayou that paralleled the Mississippi River–and years earlier had been part of the river. The bayou was a major artery of transport: "The longest street in the world," some had said. It was always busy with shrimp boats, house boats, and tugs. Boats that serviced the oil rigs in the Gulf added to the traffic.

First Baptist Church of Golden Meadow was a small,

wood-frame edifice a couple blocks off the Bayou. I was now old enough to stand beside Dad as he shook hands and greeted the small congregation as they left the service. After a few months, we left Golden Meadow; it was many years later before Dad told me why. He had practiced praying for the sick with laying on hands and anointing with oil. That was controversial; the leadership asked him to resign.

We returned to a suburb of New Orleans, where we lived in a basement apartment in First Baptist Church of Algiers. World War II had broken out by then, and there was rationing of various necessities and air raid practice drills. The top half of car headlights were blacked out, parts were hard to get, and Dad's '35 Ford had to be pushed off to get it started.

> **Dad had practiced laying on hands and anointing with oil. That was controversial; the leadership asked him to resign.**

In 1942, Dad began traveling to South Alabama to preach in a rural Baptist church. In 1943, we moved, and he became its full-time pastor—and remained there for 35 years. We had moved from a house trailer in the swamp to a basement apartment in a church, and now, a "pastorium" (sort of like an aquarium, except pastors are kept in it).

Alabama was as Baptist as South Louisiana was Catholic. The church Dad pastored grew to be the largest rural church in the county, with beautiful facilities. When he finally retired, the church was virtually debt-free with approximately fifteen acres of land and well over one million dollars worth of buildings (in 1970's dollars).

> # We moved from a house trailer in the swamp to a basement apartment in a church—a "pastorium" (like an aquarium, except pastors are kept in it).

One might suppose that my journey into the ministry would be easy. Wrong! Preacher's kids see the church differently than other young people. I knew the high expectations and low wages. I knew the scrutiny of a rural community, and I also knew enough of the stresses and lack of job security. More than once, I saw Momma cry over the unkind remarks that someone made to her. It made me angry. Mother's French Catholic background made for a difficult transition into the South Alabama, rural, Baptist culture.

There were lots of reasons not to be a preacher. It would be last on my list of things to do. But the biggest reasons were my own temperament and carnal nature. I loved sports, especially football and boxing. Preachers couldn't fight back, but I could and did.

I had seen my first church fight in New Orleans, at the age of five. I knew that Christians could be nasty toward their pastor and each other. I wasn't going to take it—and I said so. But, I had a problem; I believed the Gospel and had given my life to Christ. And there was another problem; my parents had given me to God at birth.

My mid-teens were rebellious years—age seventeen was the worst. One Saturday night late, my dad said, "Son, you know what your mother and I did tonight?" "No sir." "We gave you back to God," he continued. "He gave you to us, and now, we don't know what to do with you, so we gave you back."

> **"Son, you know what your mother and I did tonight? We gave you back to God. He gave you to us, and now, we don't know what to do with you, so we gave you back."**

In spite of my attitude, I was scared of God. My parents had done the right thing, and I learned firsthand that God could handle His own business. A little over a year later, I accepted the fact that I was "called" into ministry—even more, I was "threatened." This is a very abbreviated and sanitized account of my journey into ministry. Suffice it to say, I was convinced of God's sovereignty in my life—and regardless of my preferences or circumstances, I have never doubted it.

I need to emphasize that my parents were praying people. They prayed with passion and tears. I had respect for their prayers. They had "prayed in" the groceries and the money, and "prayed through" the trials. No doubt their prayers saved my life.

I was licensed to preach in 1955, and soon began a regular Friday night meeting in a restaurant-bar that was closed for the occasion. The next year, I became interim pastor to a newly organized church and then interim pastor to another small church. And then in 1957, while still in college, I became a full-time pastor and was ordained at the age of twenty.

The church grew from 30 to more than 300 and we had a very good ratio of baptisms to membership, even though I commuted 100 miles to college. After college, I married Carolyn Dix, a beautiful Baptist girl, and we commuted the 150 miles to New Orleans Baptist Theological Seminary—while I still pastored the church.

Seminary would have been tough, even without commuting. I was taking Greek and Hebrew, commuting 1,000 miles a week, and reacting to the pernicious "neo-orthodoxy" being taught in some classes. (Neo-orthodoxy is to theology what a taxidermist is to an animal.) I had all the symptoms of a heart attack at age twenty-six. I quit before graduating and gave myself to pastoring full-time. I knew this would limit my

> **It was the "real world" that finally got to me. If I thought that getting away from seminary would solve my problem, I was mistaken. Funerals for two girls who died of cancer and a young man who committed suicide, as well as facing building problems, showed me my own spiritual lack. I would either find help or quit the ministry.**

denominational future, but my health and finances gave me little choice.

It was the "real world" that finally got to me. If I thought that getting away from seminary would solve my problem, I was mistaken. Funerals for two girls who died of various forms of cancer and a young man who committed suicide, as well as facing building problems, showed me my own spiritual lack. I would either find help or quit the ministry.

I preached expository messages and wanted the church to be Bible-based and Christ-centered. In 1964, I preached a series of messages from the book of Acts. Simultaneously, I read various testimonies and concluded that my relationship with the Holy Spirit was the issue that I needed to resolve. At the same time, my friend Ken Sumrall pastored a large Baptist church in Pensacola, Florida, and was baptized in the Holy

Spirit. He was subsequently fired because of that experience and began a new church.

The short version is that I went to one of his prayer groups in April of 1964 and received my answer—a Baptism in the Holy Spirit. Following that experience, I spoke in tongues and that became part of my prayer experience.

I did not tell the church what had happened, but from April through Autumn, we broke all our attendance and financial records. There was a spirit of revival in our meetings. Then in November, one of the deacons asked, "Brother Charles, have you ever spoken in tongues?" "Yes I have."

> **I did not tell the church what had happened, but from April through Autumn, we broke all our attendance and financial records. There was a spirit of revival in our meetings.**

He held up a small green book entitled *What Baptists Believe*. "That's not in here," he said. I held up my Bible, "But it is in here, and that is what I'm called to preach." That was the beginning of trouble. I was voted on, but won the vote and remained pastor. We lost half of the church over the next two years. Those were tough times.

Stories about me and the church left with the disgruntled members. I was called a lot of unflattering names and a "Holy

Roller." Then the denomination took up the matter and the church was voted on more times and put on probation.

In spite of it all, the church began to grow again. Methodists, Episcopalians, Presbyterians, and even Catholics came to see what was happening. I invited John Duke, a fellow Baptist Pastor, to be my associate, and I began to travel among all kinds of groups and a wide variety of venues. Then came the "Hippies" and the Jesus Movement. We filled the city theatre with special events, and hundreds of people were born again and filled with the Holy Spirit.

In the course of various conferences, I came to know and respect several other Bible teachers, including Derek Prince, Bob Mumford, Don Basham, and later, Ern Baxter. We often ministered together through the outreach of "The Holy Spirit Teaching Mission" in Fort Lauderdale, Florida. In 1969 we began publishing *New Wine* Magazine, which eventually reached 130,000 households.

Then we began a TV station, bought property, did seminars, and video tape outreaches across the U.S. and abroad. It was an exciting time, until moral problems surfaced in the life of the HSTM administrator. Don, Bob, Derek, and I made a mutual commitment to each other for personal accountability and to try to deal with the problem. We were joined in 1974 by Ern Baxter, a well known Canadian Bible teacher.

I was eight years younger than the youngest of the others,

and considered it an honor to be part of their fellowship. I moved with my family in 1971, to the Ft. Lauderdale area in order to be closer to our responsibilities, but I continued to travel. I never lost my pastor's heart even though I had resigned the local church in Mobile.

> **Other national charismatic leaders were highly suspicious of our motives and methods. Our teaching on spiritual authority, discipleship, and accountability created a fire-storm.**

"The Teachers" (as some called us) had great opportunities. Each of us had our own ministries, but together we were moving into the new ground of renewal. If I thought leaving Mobile would be the end of controversy, I was dead wrong. Other national charismatic leaders were highly suspicious of our motives and methods. Our teaching on spiritual authority, discipleship, and accountability created a fire-storm. (I recommend Dr. David Moore's book, *The Shepherding Movement* for an accurate historical account of those years.)

We also developed relationships with other leaders from Lutheran, Catholic, and Non-Denominational backgrounds. We sponsored joint conferences of leaders, and general meetings that culminated in 50,000 people gathering at Arrowhead

Stadium in Kansas City in 1977.

That year "The Teachers" traveled together with Cardinal Suenans to Belgium, Italy, and Israel. In Rome, we attended a papal audience where the Pope introduced us to his general audience as his "Ecumenical Brethren." We continued working together through turbulent times until Derek left to pursue his own ministry in 1983. The rest of us dissolved our committed relationship in 1986. That was a very painful season.

Psalm 105:19 comes to mind, "The Word of the Lord tested him." We believed that what the Lord was saying caused us to be tested. The tests have never stopped. I am also reminded of the three Hebrew youths that were cast into the fiery furnace. A fourth one walked with them—He was "like the Son of God."

When the three Hebrews were taken out of the fire, the smell of smoke was not on them. I trust that I will be as "free of smoke" as they were. Out of those and other experiences have come principles that have established me, through my own errors and successes. I am grateful to those who have tested us. It has caused some things to burn up and others to become like pure gold.

> Psalm 105:19 comes to mind, "The Word of the Lord tested him." We believed that what the Lord was saying caused us to be tested. Tests have never stopped.

That's some of my journey from the bayous of Louisiana to the Ancient Temple of Rome. But my primary focus now is the journey the Church is making on its way to maturity, and hopefully, to unity under Christ's Lordship. May God use all of our journeys to redeem us from ourselves and our own ways.

> **The world has changed in indescribeable ways since my days in South Louisiana. Will the Church be able to meet its great challenge?**

At this stage of my life, there is little concern for my own future. My wife suffered from a serious form of cancer for three years, and passed away in early 2008. Our three children are all in some form of ministry, and I am well-supported by loyal brothers and sisters in Christ. My concern is for the future, our grandchildren (both natural and spiritual), and the larger church. The world has changed in indescribable ways since my days in the bayous of South Louisiana. Will the Church be able to meet its great challenge? I believe that it will. I pray that what I offer in the following pages will only help it to do so.

CHAPTER TWO
The CHANGING CHURCH

DOES GOD STILL SPEAK? SOME dispensationalists would say something like this, "All we need to know is in the Bible." Other Christians would say a qualified "Yes, God still speaks." Still others talk to themselves and call it God's voice.

The Scriptures themselves say that man lives by every word that proceeds from the mouth of God (see Deuteronomy 8:3; Matthew 4:4). The Scripture also tells us, "He that has an ear, let him hear" (Revelation 2:7). Jesus said, "My sheep hear my voice" (John 10). There are a multitude of references in the Bible to God speaking and our hearing—His Word imparts life and light to our path. In other words, we live by hearing and believing.

The Bible is the standard for all revelation, faith, and practice, and Jesus is the model of God's will and ways. In no way do I compare what I believe that I have heard to the canon of Scripture, nor can I give heed to any thought which contradicts it. But if I believe God has spoken, I must respond in the same manner as to a verse of Scripture. I'll go a step further: without the Holy Spirit's help we cannot see into or "hear" the written word (see 1 Corinthians 2:9-10).

Would the One who created all things by His Word and sustains all things by His Word cease to be the God who speaks? Did He cease after Jesus ascended? No, the Acts and Epistles cite many instances of Him speaking. Respected leaders since biblical times have referred to occasions when God spoke to them and gave direction. Education is useful, but revelation is another thing—it is vital to our progress. Education may tell us what is already known, but revelation will lead us where we must go.

> **True revelation comes from outside the soul, circumstance, or environment...it breaks into our consciousness and changes our view or direction.**

Revelation is not soulish or psychic. Someone said, "When a psychic wins the lottery, then I will believe in psychics." But even if one did, I would not. Soul insight is different from God's Spirit speaking into time from eternity. Jeremiah 23 tells us not to back away from hearing and telling our revelation just because someone else has a false one. Revelation goes beyond speaking out of one's current culture or even some "sixth sense."

When God speaks, it energizes, quickens, and carries authority with it. "Fire" and "hammer" are two words that characterize God's Word.

True revelation comes from outside of the soul, circumstance, or environment. It comes from the Eternal Spirit who breaks into our consciousness and changes our view or direction. Often the prophet himself does not understand what he is saying because it addresses another time or place. But when God speaks, it energizes, quickens, and carries authority with it. "Fire" and "hammer" are two words that characterize God's Word. And God's Word comes to pass. A "prophet" whose words do not come to pass should not be respected.

The prophets were called to write or have others write their words. But reading what they wrote will seldom produce the impact that the voice of God had upon them. Do I therefore minimize the written word? No. It preserves the spoken word of God which is full of majesty, breaks mighty cedars, divides the fire, shakes the wilderness, makes deer give birth, and on and on (see Psalm 29).

I could go out to the trees, the wilderness, or a deer and read Psalm 29 to them. It would not have the same effect. It is the voice of the Lord that causes such results. He not only sent the world a letter; He spoke to it. And He still does. Our task is to listen, hear, and obey.

Luther had such a moment when he read verses that he had read many times before. He was deeply concerned about his own salvation and the corruption that he had seen in Rome. Then he read, "The just shall live by his faith" (see Habakkuk 2:4; Romans 1:17). The written word became God's voice— Luther "heard", and its impact changed both Luther and history. There was a timing to this word. It was always there, but the "fullness of time" had come for him to hear. Then he went on to "hear" about the priesthood of the believer and the sole authority of the Bible.

> **Unless what we have heard is confirmed with what the Scriptures say, then we should discard it.**

Unless what we have heard is confirmed with what the Scriptures say, then we should discard it. What the Holy Spirit speaks to us personally is not a "private revelation." It will be confirmed biblically and with others who hear. Our revelations do not add to the canon of Scripture, they come from it or are confirmed by it.

I would add another factor in Luther's revelation—God's self-disclosure to him, and that is this: God has a plan for the Church, and He will not leave it in darkness. He will speak at the appointed time. And as in the Reformation, He will speak the same thing to many others.

Was the Reformation the last transforming word to the Church?

This brings me to the next question: was the Reformation the last transforming word to the Church? I should point out that there was also counter-reform within Roman Catholicism. But did reform stop 400 years ago? If not, was the continuing change due to practical leaders or was it due to the voice of God? I believe the latter, and more hearing is due; it is incumbent upon us now.

The Church is in dire need of less discussion or theories about revelation and much more of His powerful Sovereign voice.

In no way would I compare myself to Luther, Calvin, Knox, or the others. But I would dare to give a personal illustration that significantly changed my worldview, eschatology, and ecclesiology. The outworking of this story goes on in my life—even now, more than 40 years later.

It was 1966, and I was in a prayer meeting in a room over a two-car garage in Nederland, Texas, at the home of a man named Casey Jones. It had been a powerful time, and several people had been filled with the Holy Spirit. Everyone had left the room except one other man and me. We sat still in awe of God's presence—an "afterglow." I wondered what God was doing to me, a Southern Baptist, fundamental, dispensational minister. My view of the future had been "rapture," not "restoration."

> **In the quietness and sobriety of the moment, I heard this: "I will restore the Church; things lost LAST will be restored first, things lost FIRST will be restored last. You will see this in the story of the Prodigal son." ...The words were exploding in my heart.**

In the quietness and sobriety of that timeless moment, I heard this: "I will restore the Church; things lost last will be restored first, things lost first will be restored last. You will see this in the story of the Prodigal Son."

The impact was immediate; I leaped from the place I was

sitting. The other man asked, "What is it?"

I could not explain, the words were still exploding in my heart. This came from outside my world and world-view. I had preached a year from the book of Revelation, six months from Daniel, and three months from Ezekiel. In Ezekiel, I had come to realize that I didn't have all the answers. I quit the series. But I had remained a "rapturist," not a "restorationist"— until that moment, and then my perspective changed.

I was driven to Luke 15 and the three parables there: the Lost Sheep, the Lost Coin, and the Lost Son. In each case, something valuable was lost, restored, and celebrated. I came to believe that the Church would be restored as well. The Church was the "younger brother" who had gone into a "far country" and traded spiritual wealth for political power and temporal wealth but was left in spiritual poverty; it was "coming to itself" and going home to Father's house.

The first thing lost in the Church was apostolic unity and I believe it will be the last thing regained.

Restoration is not a new view of the Church— it was simply new to me. But the implications are beyond what any of us know. Much of the Church has acquired a view of salvation based on faith, and that has been regained. But the first thing lost in the Church was apostolic unity and I believe it will be the last thing regained. Also lost early on was an ecclesiology or view of the church structure that released the Gospel. For many years, most churches have been in a containment mode. (And that will be much of our subject throughout this book.)

The Reformation came at a low point in the church's theology and integrity. But reform was "new wine in old bottles." Ever since that time, the bottles have been ripping apart under the pressure of revelation—confirmed in Scripture. From this point on, I began to see restoration everywhere in the Bible and in Church history.

No "old bottle" can contain the Holy Spirit or the Truth. Now we have thousands of denominations and sometimes local churches are denominations of one, with their own papacy. Is this a good thing? Yes and no. Division is not good, but the realization that external structures cannot contain the inexorable purpose of God is a good thing. Does that mean we should demean or attack legitimate brothers and sisters and their efforts to serve the Head of the Church? Absolutely not! What we should do is seek the Lord, listen intently, and obey His voice. It is about the Promised Land, not criticizing yesterday.

The first reformation was mainly theological; the continuing one is ecclesiological, or about structure. Traditional ecclesiology has done much good in preserving truth, history, education, and missions. As I stated previously, I am deeply

> # Tragically, many churches have kept the form and traded away the substance, in order to be "relevant."

indebted to it as are many millions of people. The problem has been a gradual crystallization of each new "revelation," rendering the Church incapable of flexibility and adaptation. Location, laity, clergy, and liturgy remain the focus of most churches. The form continues to look much the same regardless of theology.

Tragically, many traditional churches have kept the form and traded away the substance, in order to be "relevant." We must be faithful to the apostolic substance of the Gospel and allow God to change the form from one of containment to one of release.

Pentecostals were "restorationists" to a point. They believed in restoring the Baptism of the Holy Spirit and speaking in tongues. But they kept Evangelical eschatology, ecclesiology, and missiology. They often continued to use dispensational and fundamentalist text books. They maintained a traditional view of the Church.

Then came "Latter Rain." Latter Rain was a movement that began in Canada in 1948. They were Pentecostals who believed in restoring all of the gifts plus the offices of apostles and prophets.

But they generally kept the same view of church structure. They were precursors to the Charismatic Movement of the 1960s and 1970s (see James 5:7).

> ## The most recent phenomenon is the "megachurch" (local churches of more than 2,000 members). ...Many remain faithful to the Gospel; others do not.

The Charismatics were primarily traditional Christians who hungered for the Holy Spirit. They were joined by a variety of other groups including the "Jesus People," youth of the counter-culture. While they created home groups and communities, they eventually recreated traditional structures. I recommend the book *The Charismatic Century* by Jack Hayford and David Moore.

The Charismatic Movement began in the 1950s and 1960s (became known in the 1960s). It swept across the world quickly. In the 1970s, Charismatic issues were major topics in most denominations. But now denominations have either come to terms with these issues or the issues have died out. Charismatics for the most part have joined with others and blended in, but they left the impact of a more exuberant worship and more openness to the Holy Spirit. Sadly, some have often neglected classic theology favor of "feelology" or therapeutic approaches.

The most recent phenomenon is the "megachurch" (local churches of more than 2,000 members). There are many different types of course, but most represent a consumer user-friendly or self-help approach. These churches are efficient in time, postmodern in method, inspiring in purpose, and varied in programs that are tailored to individual needs. They are often market-driven. Many remain faithful to the Gospel; others do not.

I do not mean this to be unflattering to either the megachurch or to Wal-Mart, but in some cases they are similar: large, successful, efficient, friendly, and low-priced. As the comedian Flip Wilson would say, "It's the church of what's happening now." New megachurches are coming into being each week, but too often a personal cross is absent from the teaching.

Megachurches are similar to Wal-Mart in some ways—large, successful, efficient, and low-priced.

Unlike previous movements, most megachurches are not driven by theology or ecclesiology—though some may be. They are driven by a renewed interest in "spirituality" and the methods that tap into that interest. Americans, especially, respond to a consumer approach, though such successful churches are by no means an American phenomenon. The largest churches are outside the U.S. While faithfulness to the Gospel varies from church to church, the structure and liturgy are similar.

There is also a restorationist movement afoot, primarily outside the Megachurch Movement—It is the "Apostolic Movement." The Apostolic Movement is composed of leaders and people who seek to restore the New Testament model or ecclesiology. We certainly need apostles and prophets; we don't need more badges and titles. We do need the functions of those ministries—but the fire will prove every model and the enduring part will be valuable.

This of course is a very abbreviated account of the various movements within the larger church. Each movement is based upon what some founders believed that the Holy Spirit was saying. I believe that the history of the Church indicates that God still speaks to it, and when He does, it brings about change. Every word that God says today is rooted in the Bible and is confirmed by others who also hear it. Some do not actually hear it, but are attached to and enjoy the results. In which case, their works may not survive the tests.

The covenant that God has made with us is that His Word and His Spirit will remain with us (see Isaiah 59:21). As He keeps speaking, we will keep changing. Every new effort to obey will produce errors and casualties. But God in His grace encourages us to "get out of the boat and walk." When we fail, He will lift us up. It is an exciting process, and, as I said earlier, it is also dangerous.

One step ahead and we will be leaders. Two steps ahead and we will be pioneers. Three steps ahead and we will be "martyrs". Get moving, but be careful!

CHAPTER THREE
The FLOW *of*
LIFE

LIFE IS A RIVER THAT FLOWS OUTWARD FROM the throne of God. This is the vision that the apostle John saw (see Revelation 22). Along the River of Life grow trees that continually bear fruit. Jesus declared Himself to be the Water of Life and in the source of Abundant Life. His life is, of course, Eternal Life.

There was a river that flowed out of Eden and became four rivers that flowed to the lands of that region. Life has moved along rivers since the beginning. Rivers watered the earth and provided transportation for pioneers and merchants. Rivers and life have been bound together throughout history. Life, rivers, and blessings flow outward or cease flowing (see Genesis 12:1-3).

God breathed into Adam the "breath of life". And wind or breath is also the origin of life. "Those born of the Spirit are like the wind," Jesus said. Like water, the wind flows. The breath of God, like the water from the throne, is pure, alive, and life-giving as it flows. The "Breath of God" is in fact the Holy Spirit.

Adam's sin introduced a "death gene" into human life. As a result, we are born dying, and, while we live, we live a limited existence. Jesus came to re-introduce us to life from the throne—a life that overcomes sin and death, and flows out-

Structure is not the answer for spiritual drought. We cannot go to new forms instead of renewed relationship to God.

ward, producing fruit.

Flowing waters purify themselves; contained water becomes polluted. Many Christians live around contained waters instead of along flowing waters, and many other Christians live where the waters have evaporated. These people have become "dried out" for want of water. Some of them are thirsty for new streams.

Structure does not produce water. It may contain or even guide the path of the flow, but structure is not the answer for spiritual drought. The Holy Spirit that flows from the throne is the source of life. And when we go to new forms instead of renewed relationship to God in Christ, we err. When we begin in the Spirit, but then seek to contain what He did through some methods, we also err. Once the structure or formula becomes the focus of energy, the life begins to evaporate.

My father pastored his last congregation, as I stated earlier, for 35 years. Upon his retirement he was old, tired, poor, and felt rejected. The life had gone out of him. He had given himself to building a successful church with hundreds of members and property worth over a million dollars. In the end, they gave him flowers. Some of the leaders helped him and Mom to remodel the small cottage into which they would move.

Many of God's servants give themselves to build something that devours their lives, only to leave it to someone else who may or may not honor them or bless them afterward. They become discarded fathers.

I was angry at the church that I grew up in and that he had pastored. I knew his and Mom's devotion and love for the people of that community. He said to me, "Charles, don't be angry, I am the one who taught them."

He did indeed teach them many good things, but one thing that he taught them was that the structure was more important than the recognition of life—his and theirs. No, he did not ever say that, but by his tireless example and the tradition of Church history, that was the result. The institution used up the resources—his and theirs.

I am happy to say that for the next twenty years of their lives, Mom and Dad were able to enter into a new season of life and ministry and to reap rich blessings from God who is faithful. But many of God's servants are not so fortunate. They give themselves to building something that devours their lives only to leave it to someone else, who may or may not honor and bless them afterward. They become discarded fathers.

What is the reason for a church's failure to bless the servants of God? Sometimes it is the minister's own fault. Often it is because we have taught that life serves the church instead of the church serving the life. Not only does that mentality cause pastoral burn-out, it burns out the core leadership of the church.

Many churches are virtually empty and the communities around them are secular and irreligious. (In some cases, Muslims buy out the old church property, especially in Europe.)

All over the world there

are magnificent structures that testify to a generation or several generations of devoted people. But many of these churches are virtually empty and the communities around them are secular and irreligious (in some cases, Muslims buy out the old church property, especially in Europe). When the ministers become lifeless and pragmatic, so does the church; it begins to atrophy. The river stops flowing, and the life dies in and around it.

Because life has ceased to flow, the Church becomes polluted, and the mission is lost. People leave angry and disappointed. Some look for life elsewhere; others simply reject the Church. In the postmortem, all kinds of causes will be suggested, usually beginning with the leaders' faults. The real reason for the death is simply that spiritual life ceased to flow. It wasn't the facilities, location, or other issues; it was that the form controlled the flow, or stopped it all together.

You may have heard the story of the Christian stranded on a deserted island who, when finally located, had built three structures.

"What is that building?" they asked. "My house," he said.
"And that one?" "My church," he replied.
"And what is that one over there?"
"Oh, that's the church I used to go to," he said.

I am not anti-building or anti-structure. What I am

ANTS, VINES AND CHURCHES

opposed to is the notion that buildings or programs are the object of our service. How can we know if that is true? It is true when more energy and resources go in than go out. We can know when it becomes our identity or when our focus is on the number rather than the quality of person being produced. We can know when we have become isolated from the world

> **We know that buildings or programs are the objects of our service when the church becomes the place to go TO rather than the place to go FROM.**

around us. We know it when the church has become the place to go to, rather than the place to go *from*. We can know that the church has lost its life when the people think that the staff are the ones who carry the mission.

The above described process has happened to virtually every renewal. This is why we need to rethink the issue of ecclesiology—what the Church is and how it functions. The Church is sometimes like the poor turtle, large or small, bound by its protective shell and often afraid to stick its neck out.

One pastor wrote a parody to the hymn "Onward Christian Soldiers": *"Like a mighty tortoise, moves the church of God. Brothers we are trodding where we've always trod."* Jesus' way of doing church reveals a church that flows in the

Spirit, taking life wherever it goes; healing, delivering, and bringing the living Word of God to the world. The life of Jesus was not only productive, it was reproductive; disciples making disciples in all nations. His Church was an Isaiah 58 and 61 church, ministering to the poor, sick, and downtrodden.

Jesus is the Seed of the Church; His life is to be reproduced in kind. His life reproduced structure *within* people. He gave life that reproduced certain genetic qualities and bore fruit. One can plant a fruit-bearing tree, but one cannot construct such a tree. Jesus' life produced internal structure in individuals, but external structure cannot produce life—not even a good structure.

> **The oil refinery was contained in a large building made of transparent glass. "It produces the world's purest oil," the guide said.**

A friend told me about a vision that he had. He saw an oil refinery contained in a large building that was made of transparent glass. A guide took him through the building; the place was as clean as a kitchen. "It produces the world's purest oil," the guide said.

"How much oil does it produce?" he asked. "Just enough to keep itself running," was the reply.

Jesus' life flowed outward abundantly; there was more than

enough for Himself and the disciples. It overcame the gates of hell. The meager flow of life we often produce does not overcome the "hell" between the pulpit and the front door. Jesus promised a well springing up from within the individual that would flow powerfully and eternally to all nations.

The flow of Divine life is not a heavy burden. In my case, I had more "ministry" than life. And that is the case with many other church leaders.

One day I read the Words of Jesus, "My yoke is easy and my burden is light". I laughed out loud. "If that is the case, where did I get this yoke from?" I wondered. I got it from my own zeal and an artificial concept of Church life. I was being driven by expectations to build the Church, but I was not being led by the Holy Spirit. The flow of Divine life is not a heavy burden. In my case, I had more "ministry" than life. And that is the case with many other church leaders.

At the age of twenty-six, I was elected to be secretary of our local Baptist Pastors Conference consisting of ninety churches. I became acquainted with the stories of many ministries who labored as I did. I saw the older men struggle to survive on low wages, high expectations, public scrutiny, no job security, and finally survive to a meager retirement. I knew that I could not endure that another forty years.

Pastoral tenure was brief on average—maybe two or three years. Long tenures were exceptional and celebrated. Competition was often intense even among the Lord's servants, and there was another problem—predecessors were not usually appreciated by successors. I also had been guilty of that. Brother Hickman had preceded me at the church that I pastored. The church had declined in his latter tenure. It was easy to see his faults, and I believed that I could do better. Indeed, I led the church to grow, but I did not understand the law of sowing and reaping. After I left the church, my successor repeated my failure to honor what had gone on before him. Then finally, when my successor finally left, it happened again.

I have often regretted my failure to understand my predecessor, Brother Hickman. He was a good man who loved the Lord. But he was like so many of God's servants who are caught up in a concept of church that is not a spiritual family. I failed to realize that he was not only a minister, he was my brother. I was doing church the way I had seen others do it and the way I understood it, but something was wrong with me and with the way I did it.

Desperation creates hunger and drives us to God. I was a very negative and dissatisfied

Desperation creates hunger and drives us to God.

person; seminary had not helped my mentality toward church. My wife, Carolyn, and I attended together. The highlight was Missions Week. The secretary of the Southern Baptist Foreign Mission Board was the speaker for the week. His words touched me deeply. At the close of one of the chapel services, I was so moved that I was prepared to ask Carolyn to go with me to dedicate ourselves to become missionaries. As I took her hand and prepared to speak to her, the Lord stopped me with these words, "You do not yet know what the Church is." Since that moment, I have wanted to know.

The Church is many things; it is especially a great mystery. It is the life of Jesus flowing through those born of His Spirit. It is His Body doing His will and sharing His redeeming love. The question is what I am serving? Am I giving His life to life-givers? Or, am I spending my time on problem people and trying to build a structure? These are questions that each of us have to personally answer.

The Church is an instrument. It is a conduit and not a reservoir or theatre. It is a mission. It is not management and maintenance. It's not simply a worship service; it is the service of worship. The pressure of redefinition is upon us. The life of Jesus cannot be contained in an increasingly aging "wine skin."

There is a proliferation of "para church" ministries; this is a good thing. Christians are forming teams to feed the hungry, go to prisons, care for orphans, to build houses, reach men, and numerous other expressions of the love of God. I wonder if "para church" is the wrong label. This is more an expression of church than much of what is being done in the name of church.

These are the real fruit bearing trees by the River of Life—"their leaves heal nations" (see Revelation 22:2).

It is not law or methods that will bring the Church to its maturity. Those who believe that more law in the Church or in culture is the answer are incorrect. Had law been the answer, the Cross would not have been necessary. The real answers are internal changes, not external structures. Other leaders believe more high-tech or post-modern methods are the solution. Ours is a culture afflicted with attention deficit disorder. So we must reach them with sound bites, slogans, and special effects. Cute as those approaches may be, they are not life. They may serve as

> **Ours is a culture afflicted with attention deficit disorder. So we must reach them with sound bites, slogans, and special effects. But the question remains, "is the content of our structure the life of the Holy Spirit and the Word of God?"**

useful bait. I have no problem with changing the label or "jazz-ing up" the image. The question remains, is the content of our structure the life of the Holy Spirit and the Word of God?

I listened to Billy Graham as he was interviewed on television, and the host asked, "I guess things have changed a lot since you began your ministry." Graham answered, "Not really, the human heart has not changed, and we still need to be saved from our sins."

Sin is looking for life in all the wrong places. It is being led by our appetites instead of by the Holy Spirit. The apostle Paul reveals his struggle in Romans 7. But in Romans 8 he said, "The mind set on the Spirit is life and peace." The human need is still the same: we must be saved from ourselves. The answer to that need is in the Holy Spirit and the Word of God. The real church is the one that serves the life of Christ in both word and spirit, to a needy world.

The Bible and Church history give us valuable creeds and points of reference. "If we lose our history, we will lose our future," to quote Churchill. But both creeds and history will be lost to those who see themselves as a reservoir and not a river.

A sports figure recently said, "If we live in the past, we will lose in the present." We can only keep our history if we stay related to the Source of Life and devoted to His mission. Whatever structure the flow of life creates, it will serve the purpose of God in the world. That is the ultimate measure of success.

CHAPTER FOUR

FLOWERPOTS
and VINES

ONE DAY I WAS OUT ON THE PATIO WRITING. I paused to observe the flowers that my wife had planted in flower pots. They were naturally beautiful. But to see the beauty, I had to be there. The plants were stationery—not going anywhere. They did add beauty, ambiance, and fragrance, but you could only enjoy it only if you visited that location.

As I meditated on the scene, I thought of the Church; beautiful in season but bound to a location. It added beauty, ambiance, and sometimes nice fragrance. But you had to be there to experience it. It definitely decorates any community.

I thought perhaps some churches should be called "First Flower Pot Church." They just sit there saying, "Come see us, we are beautiful, and we smell good, too." Of course, some flowers are artificial so they don't smell; but you don't have to go through the trouble to weed, water, and prune them. And, bugs won't touch them!

In contrast, I wondered, "What has God planted?" How is it structured? Then I thought of Psalm 80. God planted a vine in the land. He made room for it and caused it to take deep root; it filled the land and covered the hills and mighty cedars. It sent out its boughs to the sea, and its branches to the river (see Psalm 80:8-11).

Vines are opportunistic. Some are virtually unstoppable. Put kudzu in a flower pot and in a few hours you won't see the pot again. Now that's church!

Vines are opportunistic. Some vines are virtually unstoppable. They come to a fence and grow over it. They come to a tree and climb it. They come to a hill and cover it, always putting down roots and sending out shoots. It is a genetic predisposition. All this goes on while another plant is bound by its own predisposition to a container.

We have a vine in the Southeastern U.S. called, "kudzu."

Kudzu comes from Japan and was brought here to stop soil erosion. I am not sure if it worked because it grew so fast, people never saw the surface of the earth again.

Sometimes it grows more than one foot per day and it has been here for years. Leave your farm a few days and your barn will have kudzu, like an octopus reaching its tentacles to devour and digest it. Perhaps I'm exaggerating a little! But put kudzu in a flower pot and in a few hours you won't see the pot again. Now that's church!

Jesus is the Branch. Isaiah, Jeremiah, and Zechariah all call Him that. The Branch of what? A family tree. He is the "Branch of the Father, of Abraham, of Jacob, of Judah, and of David." For those who study genealogy, this is apparent. He is of those family branches. And, He is the vine of which we are branches.

> **Do you see the parallel between vine and family? God is the Father of a family.**

Do you see the parallel between vine and family? God is the Father of a family. Jesus is His first-born, equal with God, and eternal. Abraham, Jacob, Judah, and David were first and foremost fathers, whatever else they were. Without their fatherhood, there would be no branches. What they produced was a family that gave us Jesus Christ. And He came to bring many sons to glory (see Hebrews 2:10). It is His family that will cover the earth, not His institution.

Jesus produced sons (Isaiah 53:10-11; Hebrews 2:10) He gave life to those who reproduced life. He nurtured them and trained them as a Father. They grew to become His friends. One day Jesus, The Branch, said to His disciples, "I am the Vine, you are the branches."

> **"Abide in Me; abide in My love, and abide in My Word." Abide is a relational word, not a geographical word.**

Given what "the Branch" meant in the Old Covenant, this was startling and significant. They were not the Branch, but they were branches of His family that would reproduce and fill the earth. Their discipleship would be proven in bearing other sons and daughters (see John 15:16).

A disciple is a "learner". His disciples had no pattern from which to learn but Jesus' pattern. They did not follow the previous generation or tradition; they followed Jesus. Jesus took the Vine analogy from Psalm 80 to John 15.

"Fruitless disciples" would not be disciples at all. Fruitful disciples would be "pruned" in order to become more fruitful. The Life of Christ would be multiplied through them, not through the Law or temple system. "Family fruit" would fill the earth as natural family had.

Jesus told them how to accomplish this mission, "Abide in Me; abide in My love; and abide in My Word." Abide is a relational word, not a geographical word. They were to abide relationally but be sent geographically. They were given the mission to go, be fruitful, and multiply (see Genesis 1:27-28).

True Christianity is like the kudzu vine in that it relates, grows, adjusts, puts down roots, and sends out shoots. The Church has grown that way in other parts of the world. In China, a spiritual father can be imprisoned but nevertheless be regarded as the patriarch of a spiritual family numbering in the millions. The Marxist government has tried to limit the Church by organizing and institutionalizing it with the "Three-Self Church".

> **True Christianity is like the kudzu vine in that it relates, grows, adjusts, puts down roots and sends out shoots.**

The human approach is hierarchical: The Divine life approach is generational. The human approach is in vertical; the Divine approach is horizontal. One grows up, the other grows out. One stagnates into maintenance; the other multiplies with mission.

God is glorified not in what a believer joins, but in what a disciple produces. Our identity is not in our membership but in our fruitfulness. His joy and ours is in producing spiritual sons and daughters. I am a member of a local church, but my identity is in those that I have helped to produce.

One of the most disappointing sights is to see believers in

developing nations imitate the Western Church model. They begin with Spiritual power and end in a theatre model which turns their focus inward. The numbers may grow, but personal fruitfulness diminishes. The issue of personal fruit remains, and it is the best means to penetrate a hostile culture. It was Jesus' first fruit that penetrated the hostile world.

> **The apostle Paul gives us the clearest view of reproductive fruit when he says to Timothy, "Teach faithful men who will teach others also" (2 Timothy 2:2). There are four generations represented in this verse.**

Some may point to the fruit of the Spirit mentioned in Galatians 5. However, the fruit of the Spirit is the Holy Spirit's fruit in us—character. Our fruit is reproducing disciples, if one considers the commissions of Christ and the words of John 15. Had the disciples not bore that kind of spiritual fruit, we would not have received the Gospel—no matter how "spiritual" they were. True spirituality is reproductive.

The apostle Paul gives us the clearest view of reproductive fruit when he says to Timothy, "Teach faithful men who will teach others also" (see 2 Timothy 2:2). There are four generations represented in this verse: Paul, Timothy, fruitful men, and others also. The Expositors Bible's note on the verse says that his approach was typical of other apostles. Given the Great Commission, I believe that this is a correct view of apostolic practice.

Over a period of time, apostolic practice gave way to Roman Imperial structure. Church became more about location, clergy, and creeds, thus concretizing itself. While the desire to protect the integrity of the faith was good, it failed to protect the apostolic practice of bearing fruit on a personal level. The Church then grew by assimilation, infant baptism, and marriage to the political system. It eventually consisted of many people who were not regenerated, alive in Christ, or capable of fruit bearing.

The Church has grown by assimilation, infant baptism, and marriage to the political system. Eventally, it consists of many people who are not regenerated, alive in Christ, or capable of fruit bearing.

The true vine grows outward. It puts out shoots, then roots, and more shoots. My contention is that it is the individual that bears the fruit, not the corporate structures. It is that the personal responsibility of a true disciple lines up with the teaching of Jesus and the practice of the apostles. Institutional participation can have many benefits, but it is not a substitute for the personal responsibility to give freely what we have received.

I do want to underscore the importance of fighting theological error, maintaining sound teaching, and apostolic theology; in some ways the Roman Church accomplished that. But it is also fair to say that the Roman Church compromised the apostolic teaching in several areas. One of the most debilitating ways that it compromised was to leave too much power in the hands of priests and turn many of the "laity" into "spiritual dependents." This

> **People who become spiritually dependent on the Church or some false god often become disappointed and easily transfer their dependence to some other source, such as the state, as in socialism or communism.**

result corrupted the clergy in many cases, but it also greatly weakened the constituents. Poverty might be a result.

People who become spiritually dependent on the Church or some false god often become disappointed and easily transfer their dependence to some other source, such as the state, as in socialism or communism. Those who are willing to allow professional clergy to work out their salvation can be quite willing for the state to work out their economic salvation. And those who believe that poverty is a spiritual virtue might also accept it as a social and economic virtue.

Conversely, those who have been taught personal salvation by faith alone, may not accept a life of dependence and will likely apply the principle of faith and stewardship to every area of life, including finances. People of personal faith will submit to civil authority but not become dependent or look to it for resources.

The truth of this is supported by the Reformation. Wherever people gained a higher view of God and clearer view of personal salvation, the economy changed and became strong. This was especially noticeable in France where the "Huguenots" were gaining spiritual and economic growth. They were of course terribly mistreated by the state and the Church that controlled it. Those that were not killed or imprisoned took their prosperity elsewhere.

Today France is a secular nation; the Pope himself has declared it non-Christian. The Islamic minority is growing rapidly. It is highly socialistic and state-regulated. And, its acceptance of a secular world view has not freed it from a wrong view of economics. Is France's decline due in part to a wrong view of Church life? I think so.

All of this is certainly not to say that Catholics are not Christians. There are many fine Christians among Catholics and people who do have a very personal relationship with Christ. American Catholics, in particular, have generally moved beyond the pre-Reformation Catholic view of personal salvation and economics. But for all of us, any distortion in our view of God or of the Church brings a distortion into the way we live. As Van Til said, "Culture is religion externalized."

I believe that all of the Western world has suffered from the traditional view of how the Church functions. While we have seen theological reform, much of that reform has deteriorated due to a stagnant concept of structure. The way that Protestants, Pentecostals, Catholics, and Evangelicals define Church is not all that different. It remains location, clergy, laity, and liturgy. Those who think that they do not have liturgy need to review how often the form is repeated. Whatever the flower looks like, it remains mostly in the flowerpot.

> **I believe that all of the Western world has suffered from the traditional view of how the Church functions.**

There are exceptions in all groups of Christians; many people do reach out, begin ministries, and attempt to be salt and light. Sometimes they do so with the support of their leaders—sometimes without support. In any case these efforts are to be applauded and should be a model for the entire Church. I should include various Roman Catholic orders that do great social service in this applause. Mother Theresa is a prime example.

We must all face the fact that even where churches are growing in the West, there is a continual marginalization of Christianity in the face of secularism. Jesus' prayer that we be sent into the world has only been partially answered. And that part of the prayer remains unfulfilled for most individual believers. (I do not equate simply paying missionaries with fulfilling our personal responsibility to go into the world.)

> **We must all face the fact that even where churches are growing in the West, there is a continual marginalization of Christianity in the face of secularism.**

The concept of an isolated Church that is fundamentally escapist has made room for the "beasts of the field" in our civil institutions. Barbarians such as Stalin, Hitler, and Nietzsche have wrecked havoc in what should have been a harvest. Their influence has greatly affected the West.

Can we return to a vine ecclesiology, and an apostolic view of how the Church grows? I believe so, and that is already occurring in many places. Here are some suggestions for how to move in that direction.

❧ *Don't kick the flowerpot.* This is not about criticism, it is about bearing fruit. The purpose is not to destroy Church as we have known it, but to hear from God as to His plan for it. Bear in mind that all change is not necessarily good and positive change must be demonstrated, not merely advocated.

❧ *There is mentoring that goes on currently.* Most leaders have been mentored in some fashion. Identify where and how this is happening. Improve how mentoring is being done and look to biblical examples for that improvement. (Specifically, look at Jesus' model.)

❧ *Place more emphasis on personal fruitfulness and spend more time with fruitful people.* Spend less time in maintenance and problem solving. Encourage those who are reaching beyond the walls and recognize their efforts before the Church.

❧ *Teach the individual that is being focused upon how to relate to non-Christians in a normal way, using Jesus as the model.* Then teach them how mentoring works outside the walls.

Teach the people who are moving outward how to be filled with the Holy Spirit and how to be sensitive to Him in the process of fulfilling the Great Commission. He governs the process.

And teach the vine-oriented believer how to study the Bible and be equipped so that they will transmit authentic faith.

This is not a program or crusade to be manipulated or formularized, though those efforts have achieved some success. It should be approached as a normal part of the Christian life. It is for every true disciple. But don't focus on the ones who fail to receive it. Focus on those who do receive what we have to give.

Again, I am not advocating the destruction of the flowerpot. Some will always follow that pattern. I am advocating the planting of a vine in it or out of it. The true vine will always look outward to the world where the mission of Christ sends us. The true vine is always on a journey.

CHAPTER FIVE
THREE
WORDS

THERE ARE THREE KEY WORDS THAT I USE TO describe New Testament Church form: **organic**, **digital**, and **flexible**. And these words describe where I believe much of the Church will go in the years ahead. A vine is organic—alive—and it is digital. The life is in each cell and joint, and it is highly flexible and able to adapt to almost any surface.

ORGANIC

To a great extent, I have already discussed the organic nature of the Church. Organic simply means something that is alive, or was at one time. For our purposes, it means a person who is alive with the life of Christ (the Holy Spirit inhabits them). The Father is the source of that life: Jesus demonstrated Divine life and the Holy Spirit administrates it.

> **Once membership becomes disconnected from the life of the Spirit and from each other, the Church ceases to be organic. To the extent that it becomes disconnected, it begins to lose life and the power to reproduce.**

Life flows from the throne of God, as stated earlier, and Jesus came to give it to us abundantly. The Holy Spirit fills us with life to overflowing (see John 7:37). Christ's life is in His blood which cleanses us from self and sin, as we fellowship with Him and with one another. Wherever we are together in Him, He shows up and life is multiplied. Revelation occurs in these settings and the Word of the Lord is multiplied.

Jesus and His disciples represent the ultimate in organic ecclesiology. They are the model that has often been changed but not improved upon. (We need to remember that Jesus was not only the Son of God, but He was also intelligent.) This model was again demonstrated throughout the book of Acts from beginning to end. The epistles continually call the Church back to Christ, not only theologically but ecclesiologically. He is the living substance of Church life; and He is the living form of Church life. He knew what He was doing.

Once membership becomes disconnected from the life of the Spirit and from each other, the Church ceases to be organic. Or, to the extent that it becomes disconnected, it begins to lose life and the power to reproduce. It may reproduce churches but not disciples. The Church then depends upon its structure or its programs or how well it does meetings for growth. It becomes a theatre, with a cafeteria attached.

All the life that we see around us, plant and animal, are a testimony to the reproductive urge that life gives. The small ant or the bee in their protective ferocity tell us that life both reproduces and protects its progeny.

> **The small ant or the bee in their protective ferocity tell us that life both reproduces and protects its progeny.**

The ant will die for the queen who lays the eggs and so it is with other animal life. The gene pool requires it. There is a "genetic covenant" to protect and multiply the species.

When "Christians" lack this covenant of life and the urge to reproduce, are they legitimately Christian? If the motivation to "win souls" is not internal, are they genuinely New Covenant believers? Is the "spiritual consumer" motive a legitimate one?

Does that not nullify the organic motive to reproduce? That urge is a true sign of life, whether Catholic, Protestant, or Evangelical. The absence of the reproductive motive is a bad sign in any context.

Organic faith and community is one in which each person enjoys the life of the Holy Spirit, the family, and the mutual desire to multiply—the creative urge. Each person is a tributary in the river of life that flows from that community to the world.

Evangelicals, Protestants, and Catholics insist that communicants have some experience with the Holy Spirit. Yet, the percentage of people who reproduce in most cases is very small. So where is the problem? In many instances there was no real

> **The purpose of God is invested in future generations who must be prepared to receive His unfolding plan and implement it. The contemporary Church is failing in this regard, We are losing our youth to secular education, drugs, alcohol, sexual promiscuity, and violence.**

experience with the person of Christ or the Holy Spirit. In other cases they were imprisoned or made impotent by a false concept and culture of Church.

Life not only aspires to reproduce but to reproduce better

specimens in the next generation. Most human parents demonstrate this desire. The natural urge is to prepare for the successive generation. This is clearly the teaching of the Scripture in places like Genesis 18:19 where future generations would fulfill the promises to Father Abraham. It is also in Psalm 78 as fathers were taught to pass on the accumulated wisdom of forefathers. The purpose of God is invested in future generations who must be prepared to receive the unfolding plan and implement it. The contemporary Church is failing in this regard. We are losing our youth to secular education, drugs, alcohol, sexual promiscuity, and violence.

The greatest joy of old age is not in accumulation but in passing on to good stewards what we have received. The joy of the Lord, I believe, is in reproductive effort and being good stewards of the life we received by transmitting it to the next generation. Success is in having prepared successors. At this point, natural and spiritual life agree, as do natural and spiritual principles in general.

Natural life moves us not only to reproduce, but moves us to support what we reproduce until it is capable of reproducing and supporting a third generation: for instance, Abraham, Isaac, and Jacob's generations. Having accomplished that, then we can "go home" in peace. So it should be in spiritual life. This is what I mean by "the Church is organic."

DIGITAL

The second key word that I will present is "digital." The Church is digital. You will quickly realize that I am not a "techie," but all of us know that there is a digital revolution. We have moved from mechanized parts that make one whole, to individual units that themselves are whole. We have moved from machines to microchips and digits.

Many years ago a friend worked at the Oak Ridge Computer that had assisted in the development of the atomic bomb. He took me on a tour of that very large computer. It was the size of a small warehouse and consisted of large tubes connected electrically. The room was filled with a whirring sound, as information flowed from one tube to another.

The Oak Ridge Computer assisted in the development of the atomic bomb. It was the size of a small warehouse.

Later, twenty-five years after that experience, I was speaking in Canada. A young man placed in my hand a microchip that could hold more information than the entire Oak Ridge computer. I looked at it in the palm of my hand and wondered about the revolution it was causing. It was not only a technical advance; it was a sociological change that we are only beginning to fathom.

In his book *The Millennium Matrix* author Rex Miller points out that technological change produces sociological change. He describes how when society moved from oral to written communication, print to radio, radio to television, and analog to digital, societal change soon happened. The world became smaller and more connected. Railroads and planes could add to this discussion.

Thomas Friedman in *The World is Flat* offers a similar theme. He says that the discovery of a round world was sponsored by a state. Globalization of that round world was sponsored by corporations. But the digitization of the world has again "flattened" the playing field and made the world even smaller, so that individuals anywhere can participate with individuals everywhere. These individuals cannot only interact, but create ideas that change how things get done.

Digitalization is an **individualization** that stresses and refines all kinds of structures. **Individualization** is not **individualism**. The former is interactive, the latter is isolation. When I was in my twenties, I was asked to speak at a civic club. My topic was, "Christian Individualism." After I spoke, or misspoke, a kind old gentleman pointed out that my topic was an oxymoron. Individualization—or producing healthy individuals—is not individualism. Upon further thought, I agreed and felt like a plain moron. Christians are called to be mature and whole persons, but they are called to be related and interact with other Christians—not isolated.

In the late 1970s my thinking progressed and was expressed in a series called "Internal Integrity and External Integration of Structures" or "Integrity From the Inside Out!" The core idea was that healthy units integrate and find a larger identity. Unhealthy units isolate. I emphasized the mutual interdependence of personal wholeness and the corporate whole. Both the cell and the entire body have the same DNA.

About the same time I read a book, *Three Scientists and Their Gods* by Robert Wright. Wright interviewed E.O. Wilson who studied army ants. He focused upon how they were able to communicate and function with such devastating efficiency. Wilson came to conclude that they had a very high amount of common genes due to the queen and that they communicated chemically. He isolated the chemical that commanded them to bury the dead, applied it to a living ant, and the others buried it.

E.O. Wilson studied army ants. He referred to a colony as a "Super Organism." They were many who performed as one.

Wilson referred to a colony of army ants as a "Super Organism." They were many who performed as one. They shared a common nature and were able to respond to a common command. This is digitalization: small units with common life and purpose.

Do army ants give us a clue to the emerging ecclesiology? Yes, digitalization in Church life means that we reproduce healthy, whole individuals who share a common nature because they share the same King, and respond to the same Holy Spirit to fulfill our common mission—in a variety of ways.

> **How do army ants give us a clue to emerging ecclesiology?**

Back to the word integrity; it comes from a mathematical term designating a whole number which is able to fit into a larger number completely. Integrity in Church life refers to the quality of the person produced that is able to integrate. The challenge for the Church lies not in the ecumenical ideal, it is in the ability to produce healthy, secure individuals—digits. Healthy followers of Jesus share His life and the mission. Those are true disciples, who cross sectarian and social boundaries.

Digitalization will require a focus on the person that we reach and train, not merely the program that is employed. The quality of the individual person is the key to the living whole as healthy cells are the key to healthy body. Managing structure will not in itself succeed in this necessary effort. Pastoral leadership must focus on the individual, not to control, but to mentor and reproduce mentors. The focus on quantity rather than discipleship is misplaced. The more pastors become managers, the more they cease to be mentors. The measure of our labor is in the maturity and reproductivity of our disciples as was the case with Jesus.

> **The more pastors become managers, the more they cease to be mentors.**

Yes, digitalization is an ideal and idealistic when it comes to Church life. However, every achievement was once an ideal. Technologically speaking, digitalization is no longer an ideal; it is a reality. Ecclesiologically speaking, digitalization was a reality in Jesus' Church and it will be once again. And that will be necessary if we are to achieve the third word: flexibility.

FLEXIBILITY

The weakness of analog technology is inflexibility. The part can only do one thing. Institutional thinking, likewise, is inflexible; it cannot meet the changing needs of society. Digitalization has produced rapid flexibility. The individual unit responds to many different commands and configurations. It is both command and need responsive. It does not have to change its shape or substance to fit into a different environment or solve a different problem.

> **Relevance is a large issue in today's Church. In pursuit of relevance, many groups have sacrificed integrity in the presentation of the Gospel. The failure lies in relating to individuals on a CONSUMER basis rather than a MISSION basis.**

Flexibility means that we can adjust without compromising our integrity. We can adjust **because** of our integrity. In other words, the person is the same at church or at the factory, school, office, or craft. The character and principles of Christ are the same in every environment.

Relevance is a large issue in today's Church. In pursuit of relevance, many groups have sacrificed their integrity in the presentation of the Gospel. Others have used postmodern methods to accomplish relevance. The failure lies in that they frequently relate to individuals on a **consumer** or experience basis rather than a **mission** basis. The effect is a person who may love to "do church" a particular way, but fails to embrace the Cross, the Holy Spirit, or the mission. When they leave the meeting, they have not been equipped to function in what is often a hostile environment. They may "witness" but fail to be a witness. Their best effort at evangelism is usually, "Please come to my church."

The inflexibility of the traditional Church should be evident to all of us. It is not coping very well either with the mission or the environment. Even when a particular church becomes large, as some are, it is usually gaining from its entertaining ability or pastor's personality. It is not greatly affecting culture through mature disciples. Notice that the cultural statistics for cities with many churches or large churches are similar to cities with fewer churches. I conclude that the "Light" is in the meeting not in the world.

I recently heard Joel Osteen, pastor of the nation's largest church, advocate that individuals find friends who could mentor them in order to grow. I found that encouraging.

> **In the early days of my attempt to make disciples, I'm afraid that I took more of a "cookie stamping" approach— "one size fits all." But one size doesn't fit all.**

Again, there are exceptions. I have no criticism for growth as long as the individuals themselves are growing, and as long as the growth is being produced in the "street." Sunday should be a celebration of Monday through Saturday, not an isolated relief from Monday through Saturday.

In the early days of my attempt to make disciples, I'm afraid that I took more of a "cookie stamping" approach—"one size fits all." But one size doesn't fit all. God created people with different capacities and abilities. Our task is to not to make them all alike, or become apostles, prophets, pastors, teachers, or evangelists. It is to help them to discover and become equipped, to fulfill their own God-given purpose. There will be common principles employed to accomplish this, but a variety of outcomes. Real mentoring helps the individual to find his or her own voice.

For instance, I pastor a number of different leaders. Some of them I trained or helped to train. Others came to me already mature and functioning. Some of these people are pastors and some are in business or professions. There are two who work in restorative ministries, encouraging people whose lives have been devastated in one way or another. One works in radio and another works with political leaders abroad. Some are apostolic, other evangelistic, and some are missionaries.

> **Real mentoring helps the individual to find his or her own voice.**

The point is, they all share a common "DNA"—a common sensitivity to the Holy Spirit, and they all have integrity. But they each have a personal calling and can function in a variety of environments. Whenever there is a serious need, these people can rally their resources and focus their efforts together.

Organic life and digital development have produced flexibility in fulfilling our common mission. One of the men that I pastor is a dentist who also pastors a local church. That church has birthed more than 30 ministries to the community. They include feeding the hungry and restoring addicts and prostitutes.

These outreaches were not born out of a focus on meetings, but rather a focus on service. Because of that church's service, the pastor was selected as "Man of the Year" by the city leaders where he ministers. He led the church to become involved at the personal level.

> **Church, like school, is a group activity, but the measure of success is personal. Many Christians never graduate into real world success.**

Church, like school, is a group activity, but the measure of its success is personal. Each "student" is tested and measured. Evaluation of both church and school depends upon what is achieved afterward. Students who stay in school all their lives without ever becoming productive have in fact failed. Many Christians never graduate into real world success.

The student has to take responsibility for putting lessons into practice. But, I wonder if the mentor bears some responsibility for clear enunciation of the purpose of education. Is knowledge the goal or is it the means to a goal? For the disciples of Jesus it was the means. Personal and corporate missions were the goal. They were spiritually alive, personally empowered, and highly flexible. They permeated the most hostile cultures and changed those cultures. It will happen again.

REVIEW

Let's take a moment to review what has been said. My purpose is to address church structure and where I believe that much of it will go. I have suggested that it is not an easy journey toward the call of Christ, and it may even be dangerous. To fulfill His call we must keep our eyes on Him.

In order to help you understand the issues that I pose, I have begun with a brief account of my own journey through Church life. It has been one of great variety and controversy. And I have often erred in my effort to apprehend what I was apprehended to do. Hopefully, my errors and successes can be useful to others.

One of the key points of this presentation is that the Church is continuing to reform. The first reformation was mainly theological; the ongoing one is ecclesiological or structural. I shared a vision that changed my perspective in 1966. I attempted to give a brief overview of Church history which supports that vision and how the Church will return to apostolic structure.

A fundamental part of my thesis is that life will ultimately determine structure, not the reverse. Life is like a river that flows and determines its own path. Wherever the attempt is to

simply control or contain that life, the quality of life deterio-
rates. We need to see the Church as releasing life rather than
containing it.

An illustration of this concept of releasing life is presented
in the chapter on "Flower Pots and Vines." I am advocating a
"vine ecclesiology" that reaches out, rather than a hierarchy that
reaches up. A vine ecclesiology is generational and reproductive, rather than vertical and managerial.

I suggested three words that characterize biblical ecclesiology: organic, digital, and flexible. Organic refers to the life
that is in it and determines its nature. Digital is the person it
produces; flexible is the way it functions in the world. I went
on to offer examples of how I have seen these three words
operate in those I pastor.

In the next sections, we will discuss spheres of leadership,
how they are developed, how they are led, and how they grow.
We will talk about connecting with people—and specifically
men. And I'll be so bold as to talk about the flow of money.

The concluding chapter will deal with the wonderful mystery of fellowship and how Jesus meets us there. It brings a
measure of the Divine and heaven itself into our earthly mission. So, if you are ready, let's get to the "nuts and bolts" of the
emerging ecclesiology—how we "do church." The rest of the
Church trip can be scary, but very rewarding. Don't these
words, "scary" and "rewarding", usually go together?

CHAPTER SIX

KNOW *YOUR*
SPHERE

BY SPHERE I MEAN, ***WHO*** DO YOU ACTUALLY lead—not *what*. I had known my "sphere" for 14 years—it was a Southern Baptist congregation in Mobile, Alabama; it was *what* I led. But in 1971, I moved to Ft. Lauderdale, Florida, to be near other teachers and responsibilities with which I had become associated. We were doing seminars, publishing a magazine, making videos, building a TV station, running a tape library, and conducting a regular local gathering.

I wanted to leave Mobile, not only to join my fellow teachers in Ft. Lauderdale, but to make room for my successor in Mobile. I had led the church there for fourteen years; the last seven years I had led it into the charismatic dimension. I knew that separation would be difficult, and it proved to be. I had fathered many of those people in the faith, but I declined invitations to return for weddings and funerals. We only returned to visit family, with one or two exceptions.

Soon after arriving in the Ft. Lauderdale area, I was invited to pastor a local church there but declined. Then the other teachers asked me to begin a new congregation. We had several hundred locals who attended regularly scheduled Bible studies. After serious consideration, I declined "I am an uncle here, but not a father" was my response.

But my pastoral instincts and need for fellowship had not gone away. I began a house group of several families who were all close friends.

It was a transitional season for our family. We were uprooted from the culture and region where we had grown since childhood and felt very close to it. I was now thirty-five years old and deeply concerned about family and future. We had two children and another on the way.

During this season, I came across 2 Corinthians 10:12-18 where the apostle Paul writes about his sphere of leadership. He used the terms "sphere" and "measure" numerous times. In 1 Corinthians 4, he had already asserted his fatherhood of the Corinthian Church, and I began to see fatherhood as a fundamental aspect of church life.

I began to seek the Lord for my sphere as Paul had described his sphere. I was traveling thousands of miles and speaking hundreds of times, but where was my focus—my responsibility? At first I thought my sphere was geographical,

> ## Who are you responsible TO and who are you responsible FOR?

but then realized that it was not a place, but **people** that the Lord had given me to lead. (As in John 17—"those you gave me.") Then two questions developed in my mind—I believe from the Lord: "Who are you responsible **to**, and who are you responsible **for**?" The first question was clearly answered; I was responsible to the other Bible teachers. I had committed myself to a relationship and accountability two years earlier. So, I assumed that the ones I was responsible for would also become clear in a like manner, and soon they did.

"Charles, you are my spiritual father. Will you allow me to relate to you and learn? I need a pastor, will you pastor me?" These were questions that came from some that I came to believe were led to me, as I had been led to the other teachers.

I have continued through all the ensuing years to believe that God was showing to me my sphere of leadership. He spoke things to me on numerous occasions that helped me to understand that I was to lead certain leaders and specific people. It was personal.

An incident occurred earlier while I was still pastoring in Mobile that helped to define the problem of "the pastor" attempting to personally pastor all of the local church. A man and woman began attending our church among the hundreds of others. I assumed they were married to one another; in fact, they were married, but to two other people. They attended for several months, each going through the divorce process and finally marrying one another. I was shocked to discover that they had no real relationship to me or the church. They just loved the meetings.

> **I began to have nightmares about what else might be happening where I was "pastor."**

I began to have nightmares about what else might be happening where I was "pastor." I sought the Lord and I believe that He spoke, "You don't have to raise your grandchildren." It caused me to focus on raising up "other pastors within the church," but with little success. I could not escape the clergy-laity mental block in the minds of the people.

Now in Ft. Lauderdale, I did not have to contend with that mindset. I was free to allow the Lord to show me the people for whom I should and could care. I would have the grace to do this task. The Lord took me to Moses, his unbearable burden, and the counsel that Jethro gave to him, to divide the responsibility (see Exodus 18:13-27). So my thinking moved further toward only accepting a specific responsibility to pastor or mentor those for whom I could be accountable (see Hebrews 13:7, 17 and John 10:14).

I should at this point distinguish between pastoral care and mentoring (making disciples). Often these different functions are not distinguished. Mentoring is essentially personal training and is limited in duration, and is for the purpose of producing a mature person who can mentor others. Pastoring is an ongoing relationship that feeds, leads, and protects. 2 Timothy 2:2 speaks to mentoring. Acts 20:17-38 speaks to pastoral care.

> **My biggest mistakes have been made when I attempted to delegate a God-given responsibility to someone else who was not graced to bear it or when I took on a responsibility that the Lord had not given.**

As the years progressed, I ceased to directly disciple anyone else and give myself to care for those who had become leaders in some field of service. My "sphere" however, became clear in the early and mid-1970s. Since that time I have lost very few personal relationships. My biggest mistakes have been made when I attempted to delegate a God-given responsibility to someone else who was not graced to bear it or when I took on a responsibility that the Lord had not given. Thankfully, these painful experiences have been few.

Ft. Lauderdale freed me from certain concepts, but not from problems or controversy. If I had thought otherwise, I was tragically wrong. The controversial issues of authority, submission, discipleship, and small groups crossed international boundaries. Books, tapes, television, and other ministries all became part of the melee. We were accused of so many gross errors. It was a storm. Among the charges was that we had built a financial empire. I will deal with the subject of controversy more in-depth later.

What is a sphere?

So what is a sphere? It is a measure of responsibility for and to, specific people or groups of people. The responsibility in my case was for certain people—to be their pastor, and in some cases mentor. The apostle Paul's sphere included numerous leaders and churches—to serve them apostolically; he had fathered them. And as in all truly spiritual relationships, there is mutual care.

"Sphere" certainly has a larger definition as it relates to managers or professionals, but my purpose here is limited to personal experience. Church leaders have to ask themselves if they are moving toward a professional rather than a people sphere. If so, they become more and more managerial and less and less pastoral.

The call from my pastor friend went like this: "Charles, I am very concerned about what I hear you are doing." "Why?" I asked, though I knew.

One of my problems was that now I was in both traditional and non-traditional worlds and this worried my minister friends who functioned in a more traditional pastoral mode. During this season I was called by a pastor friend who had a congregation of about 10,000 people. I had ministered there on nine different occasions. It was a great honor. And, he had invited me to become part of the pastoral staff, but I declined.

The call from my pastor friend went like this: "Charles, I am very concerned about what I hear that you are doing."

"Why?" I asked, though I knew. Some of his young leaders had left him and related to one of my fellow teachers. And he had heard negative reports of what I was now doing.

He explained that my new approach to discipling would hurt my ministry. As the conversation progressed, I asked, "How many people are you baptizing in a given year?"

"About 5,000," he responded.

"How many of them will remain there with you?" I asked.

"About 1,000," he guessed.

"What happens to the other 4,000?" I pressed.

"Some go to other churches...I don't know; the Holy Spirit takes care of that."

We did not resolve our problem. I was thinking of one person; he was thinking of thousands. I was a pastor; he was a manager with evangelistic gifts. Our gifts were in conflict—but they did not need to be.

His church was very a successful multimillion dollar facility with many outreaches. His arena seated 3,500 people in a most prestigious area of California. I was operating out of my home. His was a center for Christian outreach; mine was a spiritual family. His focus was accumulation, mine was replication.

I did not feel threatened by what he was doing. I was honored to have been part of it. But it was evident that what I was doing concerned him. He invited guest ministers to speak against what I was doing and sent the tapes all over America.

This account gives a brief look at a much more broad conflict that went on in the 1970s and still does, but with less acrimony, thank God. How to enable various models to complement each other remains difficult. The issue is, how do you define **sphere**? This struggle is "messy" but necessary; it is like a birth. Transition with humans always seems to be "messy".

So, how can we know our sphere? Here are some questions; see if you can answer them:

Where has God placed me positionally

and relationally?

A pastor & discipler @ Covenant Church

Who am I accountable to? Who am I accountable for?

Bro. Billy.   Chris Clark. Family. Men's group.

What are my gifts and callings?

encouragement giving. pastoring. preaching.

What is my primary focus in ministry and who is my

primary focus?

discipling of men

Who do I actually lead or who follows when I lead?

possibly Chris. not sure   possibly no one.

Who mentored me? Am I mentoring anyone?

Larry Mullins.   Yes. Chris Clark

What is my mission? (In 20 words or less.)

To know JESUS & TO MAKE Him known

What does the kingdom of God mean to me?

(In 20 words or less.)

God's power, authority, and rule in a place and in hearts. Righteousness, Peace, & Joy in The Holy Spirit

Do I regularly give an account to anyone

for my sphere?

No

Am I training successors?

One

Can a leader be both a manager and a mentor? Absolutely. These duties are not incompatible. In most cases leaders have to do both. However, the future lies in our effectiveness at making disciples of Jesus Christ, which I believe requires personal involvement and not merely being a CEO.

I should stress one other issue: Married leaders must view their natural family as their primary sphere and model for their spiritual family. Ephesians 5, 1 Timothy 3, Titus 1, and other Scriptures draw a clear parallel between natural and spiritual family.

Good stewards know what they steward, whether gifts, callings, or people. Definition of that responsibility is essential to doing it well. This is true in business, professions, military, or any other endeavor. If we never find the ball park, we cannot play the game. If we never find the battlefield, we will never win the war. So know your sphere, that's where "it's at." Whatever it is, it is a Divine trust for which we must answer.

Where is my sphere of influence?

① My Family - *Janis Rosel Clanen Jait Mendelyn Samuel Olivia Henry Clay Marie Chris Willian Wolf*

② My Job. - Deborah Bill

③ My church -

④ My community

CHAPTER SEVEN
LEAD *YOUR*
SPHERE

LET US ASSUME NOW THAT YOU KNOW YOUR
sphere of leadership; you know whom the Lord has given to
you; you know to whom you are accountable; how you lead
those in your care, and you realize that this is a Sacred Trust. The
question is, where will you lead them?

Leadership is more than a position or managing people. It
is certainly not controlling or manipulating them. Leadership
in the kingdom of God is Spirit-led, and each believer is a
priest. Control is evidence that we do not know how to lead a
particular person.

Leadership is more than a unilateral activity in God's

Kingdom. Our leadership is affected by those who lead us and our corporate counsel resources. If we are not part of a corporate leadership, then who has authorized our action? But what must affect our direction the most is the stated, biblical purpose of God, to fill the earth with the knowledge of His Glory. We lead to that end (see Habakkuk 2:14).

It is my view that whatever I sow to those who have and do lead me is what I'll reap from those that I lead. As I give authority to those that lead me, I'll receive from those that follow me.

Real leaders put their own life on the line because they believe and are committed to their goals and course of action. And they are committed to those they lead.

What will I do with the authority that I receive and the leadership that I exercise? My own goal is to serve the call of God in their lives, to help them discover and fulfill it, and supporting them as they obey the Holy Spirit. Using leadership to fulfill personal ambitions is doomed to failure. Our leadership must be devoted to revealing Christ's Kingdom in the lives of those that we lead.

Leading by example is effective. We are not mere "pointers," but we go ahead and do what we teach. Ariel Sharon is one of the great leaders of our generation. In his book **Warrior**, he cites a time in the Yom Kippur War, when politically-appointed generals were 25 miles behind the battle line at the Suez. They were calling for retreat. Meanwhile, Sharon was leading his tanks across the Suez Canal and into Cairo, Egypt. You cannot know the battle or lead the troops from the rear; leaders go before. One pastor said, "There go my people, and I am their leader."

Real leaders put their own life on the line because they believe and are committed to their goals and course of action. And they are committed to those they lead. Menachem Begin, also an Israeli Prime Minister, was asked how he had led in battle with so few casualties. He said, "We were a family; I never planned an operation from which I did not believe

> **Good leaders demonstrate, not just advocate... character, commitment, care, vision, strategy, ability, and knowledge so that those who follow will learn how to lead.**

that everyone could return." Begin inspired trust and loyalty.

Good leaders demonstrate, not just advocate. As leaders demonstrate character, commitment, care, vision, and strategy, those who follow learn how to lead. The relationship to a good leader imparts leadership ability and knowledge.

Another important factor in leadership is principles. Jesus taught and demonstrated principles that serve the mission. There

> **Great leaders act on principles, not impulse.**

are at least twenty principles in the Sermon on the Mount. The Law as received by Moses can be understood as principles. Principles, whether followed by Christians or non-Christians, will bring good results. Spiritual principles, like laws of nature, are not prejudicial. Gravity works for everyone.

Great leaders act on principles, not impulse. I have a book entitled ***Patton's Principles***. General George Patton was an exceptional Tank Commander. He often said, "Stay on the move; never dig foxholes; they become graves." About the enemy, he also said, "Grab' em by the nose and kick them in the rear" (*rear* was not his actual expression). Of course, ***Patton's Principles*** may not work in Church life, but we all need principles that apply to what we do and how we lead.

Many leaders influence others by charisma or personality. A good personality can be a great advantage. However, when people are drawn to a person only to discover an inconsistent life, problems will be created. We impart what we have, not what we say. If we have "measles" we can preach "mumps," but measles is what they will catch. We can preach "peace", but if we are anxious, our constituents will get anxiety.

Leaders must be more than good actors, they must have substance that is fire-tested. It takes more than a "hot new method" to produce-long term results. Whatever we do must not only work for us; it must work for those who follow us.

Les Brown, a well known motivational speaker, quotes a brief poem that left its imprint upon me: "Methods are many; principles are few. Methods always change; principles never do."

My father once said that some "leaders" are always looking for a parade to jump in front of. Problem is, the parade turns away and they go marching on with no one behind them. As John Maxwell says, "They are not leading, just taking a walk."

Leaders often become captured by their constituents. They begin a movement; it becomes their identity. When they realize that changes need to be made, they fear their followers, and they perhaps should. People in general do not like change. What they fear, they fight.

Someone else said, "Leadership is like a 'flat bed' truck. A hard turn can cause your load to fall off."

Leaders impart what they HAVE, not what they SAY.

Corporeity, spiritual sensitivity, example, character, commitment, and sound principles are all vital to leading one's sphere of responsibility. An important thing to remember is that you will likely be together a long time, and your future depends upon theirs.

THE FOLLOWING IS A LIST OF PRINCIPLES THAT I HOLD DEAR:

CONSISTENCY: The Bible often calls this "steadfastness" or "unchangingness," when referring to God. Fickle and moody leadership confuse followers. Leaders need to be predictable and calm even in storms. They are the "True North" in

▌Maturity is required in a good leader.

the compass of a follower. They are an anchor to the person who would otherwise drift. Maturity removes the childishness of infancy or the mood swings of adolescence, and maturity is required in a good leader. The Scripture warns against novice leaders. God and His Kingdom are unshakeable. The more like Him a leader is, the more consistency is evident.

▌The "pure in heart" will see God.

A PURE HEART: The Bible has a lot to say about the heart, the seat of our motivations: the well-spring of our thoughts. It is to be kept like a garden—put good seed in, and keep bad seed out. The enemy's first priority is to pollute the heart; it is the primary battle ground. Jesus said the "pure in heart" will see God. The heart is naturally wicked and needs purification and constant care (see Psalm. 51). Cain failed to guard his heart and Essau allowed bitterness into his heart.

Our salvation is based upon His faithfulness to us, and our faithfulness demonstrates His salvation to those who follow us.

FAITHFULNESS: We have no word which fully communicates God's faithfulness—we simply say, "Great is Thy faithfulness!" The Hebrew word describes God's ability to be faithful to the unfaithful, because of who He is, and not who they are. His faithfulness reveals His love and grace and meets our need. His faithfulness goes beyond our worthiness.

The Scripture promises that faithfulness brings increase: Faithfulness in a little, given much; faithful in what belongs to another, given our own; faithfulness in money, given true riches (see Luke 16:10-12).

Our salvation is based upon His faithfulness to us, and our faithfulness demonstrates His salvation to those who follow us. The Prodigal's father is an example of faithfulness to a wayward son. If God has given us people who sometimes are unfaithful to us, we must decide if we will respond as God does or as they do?

SOWING: Sowing is a vital principle for long-term lead-

> **We reap what we sow; we reap in proportion to how much we sow, and we generally reap where we sow. This is both a natural and spiritual law.**

ership. We sow before we reap; we give before we receive. My father used to tell me, "If you want to accomplish something, sow it into the hearts of the people for awhile, then let it lay there. Wait for a season, then it will begin to come up in them. They will think it was their idea and you will not be able to stop them."

We reap what we sow; we reap in proportion to how much we sow, and we generally reap where we sow. The Scriptures say, "God is not mocked, what a man sows, that is what he will reap" (see Galatians 6:7). This is both natural and spiritual law.

My personal testimony is Psalms 126:5-6: I'll let you read it.

My definition of spiritual sowing is simple: Giving away the truth in love, sacrificially, with no expectation except confidence in the Lord and His Word.

MERCY: "Blessed are the merciful, for they shall obtain mercy" (see Matthew 5:7). If one truly believes this principle,

A merciful leader will have merciful followers.

then he or she will look for the occasion to show mercy. Mercy triumphs over judgment (see James 2:13). A merciful leader will have merciful followers and receive mercy from them. The reverse is also true, if we lack mercy we will reap that too. I urge useful study of Isaiah 58-61.

RELY ON THE HOLY SPIRIT: "It is not by might or by power, but by my Spirit says the Lord" (see Zechariah 4:6). Apostolic leaders, while employing principles, were empowered by the Holy Spirit. The supranatural element cannot be ignored.

"It is not by might or by power, but by my Spirit says the Lord" (Zechariah 4:6).

Principles are not prejudiced; they will work for anyone, believer in Christ or not. But as Christian leaders we must have a distinctly supranatural element—miracles should follow us as we obey God—"If God is for us who could be against us?"

Key Principles:
- **CONSISTENCY**
- **A PURE HEART**
- **FAITHFULNESS**
- **SOWING**
- **MERCY**
- **RELIANCE ON THE HOLY SPIRIT**

CHAPTER EIGHT
INCREASING
YOUR
SPHERE

NOW WE COME TO THE ISSUE OF GROWTH.
Once we know our sphere and decide on the principles that will
guide us, how will we grow the measure of our leadership?
Should we expect to grow? Absolutely.

The kingdom of God is an ever-increasing sphere, it is
always expanding (see Isaiah 9:6-7). As a defined and accountable part of His Kingdom, we are expected to grow personally
and in leadership. The Scriptures give numerous examples of
good stewards producing increase (see Matthew 25:14-29).
The fruitless branch is cut off. Fruitfulness is evidence of true
discipleship (John 15:16). So how can we grow our sphere?

Jesus led the three, the twelve, and the seventy, but He looked beyond them to all of Israel and to the world. He taught them to look beyond the cultural and geographical barriers and see the world. He had a redemptive worldview. The book of Acts documents that the apostolic worldview included all nations. The word apostle itself means "one who is sent forth." The growth motive is inherent in the Gospel and the ministry gifts.

> **If football was played in the way many churches operate, it would be more about the huddle instead of advancing the ball....Players would be allowed to change sides in the middle of a play. Injured players would be attacked by their own teammates.**

Jesus also grew personally. He grew physically, mentally, and spiritually as a man. He learned obedience through suffering, and He grew in influence and still does. He grew numerically in followers and still does. "His truth is marching on."

"Escapist" and "little flock" thinking are a denial of the Holy Spirit and our mission to the whole world. "Maintenance" thinking ignores life's drive to reproduce and multiply. In the very beginning of human history, God commands, "Be fruitful and multiply and fill the Earth."

The Church needs a renewed mind in the area of growth. It is too wrapped up with the "barn" and neglects the field. If farmers farmed the way churches operate, they would plow in the barn, sow in the barn, pray for rain in the barn, and then pray for the barn to "catch on fire."

If football was played in the way churches operate, it would be more about the huddle instead of advancing the ball. Coaches who could produce better huddles would be chosen. Quarterbacks would be selected for personality and the way they were able to speak in the huddle. And of course players would be allowed to change sides in the middle of a play. Injured players would be attacked by their own teammates.

Victory in any endeavor begins with a mentality, then moves to a strategy.

If armies operated like Churches, "friendly fire" would be the main cause of casualties. Armies would have more meetings in the barracks and uniforms would be removed once outside.

Victory in any endeavor begins with a mentality, then moves to a strategy. Aggressive thinking is required, then aggressive action.

What are some of the issues that produce growth? How did Jesus and the apostles grow?

HERE ARE SOME MEANS TO GROWTH:

- Understand that God's motive in outreach is love. Love must move us to the world.

- Determine to grow personally through learning, practice, and association. Disciple means "learner."

- Seek a continual awareness of the Holy Spirit. The Holy Spirit gives us guidance, power, and boldness for growth.

- Study the Holy Scriptures and know the Truth.

- Have good models and study their lives and principles.

- Seek clear vision from God, and develop strategies for growth through service.

- Associate with fruitful people.

- Stay positive and avoid cynical thinking.

- Know your gifts, strengths, and weaknesses; focus on your strengths, find others who can help you overcome your weaknesses.

- Apply the Cross, seek humility, and avoid self centeredness.

- Practice God's presence in all of your life—make prayer a vital part of your daily walk with God.

- Keep healthy in food, exercise, and habits.

- Stay outward in your focus.

- Learn to see problems as opportunities.

- Do not spend too much time with problem people and don't try to solve problems that are not part of your sphere.

- Understand that service is sowing, and greatness is measured in breadth of service.

- Build relationships with those who are not yet followers of Jesus.

- As much as possible, keep conversations in faith and focus on the other person's interest.

- Take the task seriously, but not yourself. Learn to see your own errors and laugh at yourself.

- Be able to share your own testimony clearly and concisely when appropriate—but never force it on others.

- Know how to use the Scriptures to lead someone to Christ. Pray for that privilege.

- Know how to mentor and give what you have received.

- Teach those that you mentor that they are also stewards of what they have received.

- Practice financial responsibility and generosity. Money is a symbol of our attitude toward God and others.

- Pray for wisdom and learn from each experience.

As we increase in wisdom and spiritual growth, so will those who follow our leadership. There will be a limit to how many people you can lead in a direct way, or relate to personally. But your sphere will grow as they do (see 2 Corinthians 10:12-15). Sphere growth is much like growing a family; as they reproduce, your heritage multiplies. Our goal is not accumulation, but multiplication. We are not only producing "spiritual children"; we are producing "spiritual parents." If we are faithful and successful, then our spiritual children will inherit the covenant promises (see Genesis 18:19).

> **Service is using our resources to meet someone else's needs on their terms, simply because we love people as Jesus did. All that He did and taught was for service, even in death. The word "ministry" means service. Service has no further agenda than to bless. It is not a means to manipulate.**

This process is not about us, it is about the Lord's will and our progeny. If we succeed, they will bless us; if not, they will curse us, or at best forget us.

I will elaborate on the effectiveness of service. There is no more important way to bless those around us. Even the non-believer understands when one serves his or her need. Service opens the heart, it "plows" the field, and prepares for the Seed of Truth. Mother Theresa is lauded by this world for her service. Hindu India gave her a state funeral even as they persecuted other Christians. Even in her darkest years, she continued to serve.

> **Wise leaders will not want to have more than God wants to give. The requirements of greater stewardship are greater responsibilities and accountability. Ambition to grow beyond our grace to grow makes for eventual burnout.**

Jesus taught His disciples that the breadth of one's service was the measure of greatness in the kingdom of God. Service is using our resources to meet someone else's need on their terms, simply because we love people as Christ did. All that He did and taught was for service, even in death. The word ministry means service. Service has no further agenda than to bless. It is not a means to manipulate.

Jesus healed ten lepers; only one returned thanks. The ingratitude of some did not prevent Jesus' service to others. He said that it was more blessed to give than receive. Service is

God's grace in action. The measure of grace that we have received from God and give to others will determine the measure of our sphere. A sphere that is born of grace can be maintained in grace. In other words, our yoke remains easy.

God does expect growth, but there are seasons when He "prunes" or cuts away the unproductive parts of our service so that we can give life to more productive areas. Those times of pruning can look and feel discouraging. We have to say, "The Lord gives and the Lord takes away, blessed be the name of the Lord."

Wise leaders will not want to have more than God wants to give. The requirements of a greater stewardship are greater responsibilities and accountability. Ambition to grow beyond our grace to grow makes for eventual burnout.

If you are successful, everyone will want to promote you. But if you are not careful, you will find yourself on a pedestal of popularity. The irony often is that the very ones who put you there are in the mob that takes you to your cross. Then you can know "it's pruning time."

Even now, the genetic multiplication of branches is filling the earth with the knowledge of the glory of God, as the waters cover the sea.

It's the life that flows that causes the vine to grow. At some point in your life, your task will change to one of supporting what you earlier produced. The branch then becomes more sturdy, less flexible, but stronger to bear the tender shoots and the fruit. And joy then is not so much about our bearing fruit, but seeing the successive generations bear fruit.

The Lord has made us a part of the true vine. He made a covenant with the vine, that it would bless all the families of the earth. He also made a covenant that we, and our descendants would have the Spirit upon us and His Word in our mouths (see Genesis 12:1-3; Isaiah 59:21). Even now, the genetic multiplication of branches is filling the earth with the knowledge of the glory of God, as the water covers the sea. That is the vision that God has given and is confirming (see Habakkuk 2:14).

What hinders the fulfillment of the vision? What prevents our obedience? Let us examine the issue from which we hide our faces.

The CROSS AND THE KINGDOM

THE CROSS IS AT THE CENTER OF HUMAN history—the matrix of a new age. It was in the mind of God before the Earth was created. It was in the mind of Christ early in His ministry. It was in the message of Isaiah and the apostles, and is the subject of our greatest hymns. The Cross is an inescapable fact of history, the core of the Gospel, and the hope of salvation for mankind.

But as Isaiah 53:3 says, "We hid our faces from it." We employ many consumer-friendly methods and psychologies to attempt to circumvent the reality of the Cross. As the friends of Jesus sought to persuade Him to avoid Jerusalem and the Cross, so we try not to go there ourselves. But as in Jesus' experience, the Cross is the door to the Kingdom (see Matthew 16:21-25). Philippians 2:5-11 makes it clear that Jesus went down to the Cross before He went up to the Throne. And we are also told to have that same mind-set.

There are many "church doctors," and specialists who are attempting to diagnose the Church's ailments. Someone said, "They can't seem to cure our spiritual diseases." I believe that the New Testament addresses our need very succinctly in the Cross—a diagnosis we would all like to ignore. We cannot have "Church" without the Cross. We sing hymns, listen to preaching, and do programs, but we still have not accomplished God's purpose. Our own way keeps getting in God's way. We must die to ourselves and our reputations.

> **What is the Cross? For Jesus it was the ultimate in self-denial, degradation, and sorrow. No one book or collection of theological minds could define the Cross of Christ.**

The problem is not the "ideal Church" or the method to get there. The problem is not the institution or the doctrine primarily. It is our "flesh." We keep trying to get to the result without the daily process of dying to ourselves. I have lived to see and experience several "waves" of the Spirit. But I have not seen a popular movement based on the Cross—His and ours. The Cross will never be popular. But it's the key to the Kingdom (see Acts 14:22).

The kingdom of God is His reign in our lives. It is within us, the work of the Holy Spirit producing righteousness, peace, and joy. What is the greatest hindrance to His reign? It is our fleshly desires. Why the Cross? The answer is obvious.

What is the Cross? For Jesus it was the ultimate in self-denial, degradation, and sorrow. No one book or collection of theological minds could define the Cross of Christ—God's Perfect Son—The Eternal Son. His Cross was unique in every manner, in that it was His, and it was for us, not Him.

It is not my purpose here to give a treatise on the Cross, atonement, or redemption. My point is that it was essential for Him and for us. To remove the Cross from the Bible is

> **It was on the Cross that God's goodness and mercy were revealed in ultimate fashion.**

to remove the Good News that we can be reconciled, redeemed, our sins removed, and have the hope of eternal life. It was on the Cross that God's goodness and mercy were revealed in ultimate fashion. He was glorified there as the One who loved us and gave His unique Son for us. It was the magnificent demon-

> **His response made no sense. His answer offered no hope for our guilt. I was deeply grieved. This was my denominational seminary.**

stration of the Father's love (see John 12:23-33).

Majestic as the Cross is, many theologians, preachers, and ordinary Christians seek to avoid it. I once took a course on the Gospels, and there was never even a mention of the Cross. Afterward, I confronted the professor, "Do you not believe in the Cross, that Jesus died there for us? Do you not believe in the substitutionary atonement—that He paid the price for our sin?"

"No," was his reply.

"What then does it mean?" I pressed.

He was unclear; "you are talking about a 'pre-millennial doctrine'," he said.

I was stunned.

He continued, "The Cross simply heightened man's guilt." Then he turned and walked away. His response made no sense. His answer offered no hope for our guilt. I was deeply grieved. This was my denominational seminary.

I went back to our small apartment, and tossed my Bible onto the couch, then fell on my knees. "Lord, if he is right, I have no message; if he is wrong, I have no business here."

When I opened my eyes the Scriptures lay open before me. My attention fell on Hebrews 9:12. "Not with the blood of goats and calves, but with His own blood He entered the most Holy place once for all, having obtained eternal redemption." Then I read the entire chapter.

Great hymns and poems have been written about the Cross as people saw the beauty of it in retrospect. But on the day it occurred, it was not beautiful. It shows God at His best, but man at his worst. That day, humanity was an angry, brutal blood-thirsty mob, crucifying everything good and innocent, heaping our sins upon Him. Some ran away and hid. Isaiah 53 says, "We hid our faces." Why? It is the sheer ugliness of the naked Savior pierced and brutalized.

> **I suspect that we are running for an innate awareness that there is also a cross for us.**

But, I suspect something else; I suspect that we are running from innate awareness that there is also a cross for us. Jesus spoke not only of His own Cross but ours (see Matthew 16:24). When Jesus prayed in the Garden, He said, "Not my will but Thine be done." He comes to express the Father's will but not His own. And that is where our cross is also, in self-denial. Such self-denial may lead and will lead to suffering. As it pleased the Father to bruise Him, it may please Him to bruise us as well, and it will not be pretty. Only later do we see the beauty of it.

No, we should not understand our cross as suffering or atoning for our own sins. Jesus did that. But as it was in Jesus' suffering that God's love and mercy were revealed, so should it be in our cross. As our flesh is humbled, His grace and glory are revealed.

The Cross is the inescapable result of the prayer "Thy will be done."

There is a multitude of testimonies to this truth. It has been said, "The blood of the martyrs is the seed of the saints." The stories of martyred or suffering missionaries, who through pain and death reached the pagan heart, are abundant. The willingness to die to ourselves allows us to serve His will, and glorify Him. His Cross is where God's glory was revealed. Our cross has the same purpose.

The Cross is the inescapable result of the prayer "Thy will be done." It was the door through which He passed to defeat hell and be glorified. Our cross, whatever it may be, is the point through which we must pass to place His will above our own, His glory above our reputation, and replace our fleshly appetites with His purpose and our zeal with His.

This is beyond self-help; it is death to self. As in Jesus' life, we do not construct our own cross; others do it for us. Jesus was wounded in the house of His friends. Our cross may be constructed there also. For Jesus, the Cross was so vital to our salvation, purification, and to our mission. Is it right to hide it from potential converts? Is it right to try to do church without it? Our greatest conflicts within the Church are the result of the Cross not applied. A Crossless Gospel will produce Kingdomless churches.

> **Our greatest conflicts within the Church are the result of the Cross not applied. A Crossless Gospel will produce Kingdomless churches.**

It was a Sunday morning in 1970, and as the congregation was leaving the auditorium, I stood at the door greeting them as they left. One of those departing offered a picture; it was simply part of an arm with the hand in the center of the picture. A nail was being driven into the wrist. The hand was open and relaxed. I took a second look, realizing what it portrayed. "That is not how I drew it the first time," the man said. "The first time I drew it, the hand was clinched. But in the night, the Lord awakened me: 'It was not that way,' He said. 'The hand was open.' Then I drew the picture you are seeing now." It had a profound effect upon me.

> **Fiery trials are those that burn away our carnal motives to personal glory. But unlike Jesus, we do not always stretch out our hands to receive the nails.**

God has called us as he called Jesus, to submit ourselves to suffering (see Isaiah 50). 1 Peter 4:12 reminds us that fiery trials are to be expected and that we should rejoice to the extent that we are made partakers of Christ's suffering; that is when His glory is revealed.

Fiery trials are those that burn away our carnal motives to personal glory. But unlike Jesus, we do not always stretch out our hands to receive the nails. I know that from my personal experiences. In 1964-1970, I was defensive about my experiences with the Holy Spirit when I was put on trial by my own church and denomination. And I was good at debate until I heard the Lord say to put down my arguments and listen. I revealed more of the Lamb of God in submission than I ever did in defense.

The years 1979-1982 were also very difficult for me. The cult leader Jim Jones had led his followers in mass suicide. The world was shocked. As I was moving my family into a new neighborhood, a local pastor published a small book accusing me and our church of having "Jim Jones-like" traits. The book was circulated through our new neighborhood.

Then the IRS began a five-year audit of our church, the most difficult kind of audit. For three-and-a-half years, we spent over $100,000 and hundreds of man-hours proving our innocence. Then, a major hurricane seriously damaged our area and our new home. After it was refinished, crosses were burned in our front lawn by people who believed the published report. I had to employ guards to protect my family and home. Our children were harassed by other the students at their school.

> **It has been said that "adversity introduces a man to himself."**

During that season, three of my teacher friends were sued by a famous doctor of psychiatry for $44 million. He had written a best-selling book. The reason for the suit was that my friends had repeated a rumor that the psychiatrist had committed suicide. That violated a California law, and he lived in California.

There were other foul winds blowing during those years, including small gatherings of religious leaders who were seeking to resolve some of the national controversy over our methods. Some of these attempts only manifested the hostility, if not exacerbating it.

I was once again discovering myself. Someone said, "Adversity introduces a man to himself." My self was not a pretty picture. I loved contact sport, having boxed and played football. Defense and offense come naturally. Once again, I was struggling with Jesus' approach to conflict.

Our oldest son, Stephen, was in high school and studying J.R.R. Tolkien's work. An animated version of **Lord of the Rings** was being shown at a local theater. "Dad, will you go with me to see **Lord of the Rings**?" he asked.

I did not want to go, but I went just to be with him. We sat in the back of the theater and watched the battles as Frodo attempted to bring the ring back to the fire. At one point, Frodo was injured by a sword. The wound appeared to heal, but he was ill with a fever. His mentor leaned over his sick body and the camera moved in for a close-up.

"Frodo, a piece of the enemy's sword has broken off inside of you; it is moving toward your heart. If it gets into your heart, you will be just like one of them."

Tears squirted from my eyes, like water pistols. I almost

cried out, "Lord please don't let it get in my heart!"

Storms pass in time and those storms also passed. The issue is, what damage has been done? Some things are blown or burned away. Among those things are motives that do not serve the kingdom of God. The Lord has promised that if we humble ourselves, He will exalt us. Humility is totally our task. Exaltation is totally His. If we humble ourselves, exaltation will not really matter. The only thing that matters is, that "the knowledge of the glory of God covers the earth and the waters cover the sea" (see Hebrews 2:14).

So what has the Cross to do with ecclesiology or how the Church works? Everything. I have loved the subject of ecclesiology and Church strategy since the 1960s, and I have read and advocated various approaches. I have been, and am, a proponent of a relational church, pastoral care, discipleship, small groups, one-to-one evangelism, and more. But I have discovered that without the Cross, the highest ideals and most ideal views

Humility is totally our task. Exaltation is totally His.

can be polluted by human zeal. A good motive can make a bad system work and a bad motive can destroy good ecclesiology.

The Cross is more than a few tough months or years. It is not a one-time experience for us. It is a daily submission to His will in all seasons—attempting to respond to life as Christ did.

I do believe that the Church will return to its origins. But between here and there lies a shadow. God help us to see the path as they saw it and respond as they did.

CHAPTER TEN
CONNECTING WITH MEN

TRUTH IS ABSOLUTE, AND IT IS THE FACTS as they exist that bothers most post-moderns. But the discovery of truth is a journey. Some search for it and never find it. We believe that Jesus is Truth made flesh and beheld in living form; He is eternally absolute. For the followers of Jesus, the search for truth begins and ends in Him.

Truth is not irrelevant when we are in crisis. Of course it is never irrelevant, but crisis makes us seek it more desperately. I was in such a moment of time in the fall of 1964. I'll share briefly about it, as it is the background for this chapter.

I had been baptized in the Holy Spirit, and did not know all of the consequences that might follow. I did know that fellow Baptist pastors had been fired for that experience and I knew that serious questions were arising in my own church. And I knew that I had a family to support.

I was not a Pentecostal, though I did not disparage their position. Nor did I understand all of the differences between my position and theirs. I did not know how to present the dimension of the Spirit to my Baptist congregation and friends. I wanted them to personally embrace the work of the Spirit which I believed to be essential. So I went away to a cabin on Mobile Bay to fast, pray, and seek the Lord.

> **I saw many women who were spiritually hungry, but not many men. God was saying, "Go straight to the problem— reach men."**

It was on the third day that the Lord spoke to me. "I have called you to be a fisher of men, as Jesus was. If you reach men, you will reach women and youth. And if you reach men, you will not have a financial problem."

I never had to write this down to remember it. It was burned into my consciousness. My mind turned to previous years when I had done a lot of counseling—mostly to women— and the topic was usually men. I also realized that currently, it was women who were seeking the Spirit and attending the

Bible studies that I taught. God was saying, "Go straight to the problem—reach men."

Some of the disciples were zealots, revolutionaries, and at least one was a crooked tax collector. These are the ones Jesus built upon.

Jesus was good at reaching strong young men. The disciples were young and masculine. Some were commercial fishermen. My father had worked with commercial fishermen; I knew that they were strong. James and John were called "Sons of Thunder" because of their bad temper. They wanted to call down fire and burn up villages that had rejected a visit from Jesus. Some of the disciples were zealots, revolutionaries, and at least one was a crooked tax collector. These are the ones that He built upon.

I never thought that Jesus looked like the artwork that portrays Him. Peter would never have invited such a person into his boat. Nor could such a person present such a powerful force as Jesus did. After all, He was the Son of God; maybe not handsome or suave, but always strong.

I saw many women who were spiritually hungry, but not many men. Believing what the Lord had spoken, I set out to reach men in order to bless women and youth. We began a

Bible study for men only. We began a softball team and I began to visit men at their place of work and try to understand their needs. I began to take groups of men out to eat for lunch and speak at men's meetings. Soon I was baptizing men.

One such man was Harold. He was well over six feet tall and large. He was a machinist. Harold visited our church because he liked to hear someone who preached the Bible the way it was written. But alas, Harold came down with a very bad back, and had to lie on the floor. He could not get up under his own power. He was on the phone:

"Brother Charles, do you believe the Bible?"

"Of course I do, Harold."

"Do you believe James 5:14-15?" he asked.

"Sure I do, what does it say?" I responded.

> I was trapped. I did believe the Bible, but had not prayed for the sick that way. I knew Harold, and that he would not take another solution.

"It says that if I am sick that I should call of the Elders and have them anoint me with oil, in the name of the Lord, and the prayer of faith will save the sick. Bring some oil over and pray for me."

I was trapped. I did believe the Bible, but had not prayed for the sick in that way. I knew Harold, and that he would not take another solution. I had no idea what sort of oil to use. I went to the pharmacy to look for oil, fearful that someone would ask why I was purchasing it. I finally settled on olive oil.

> **I looked at Harold, but he did not move. I excused myself and left feeling like a failure.**

Harold was on the floor—almost "wall-to-wall Harold." I exchanged pleasantries, but felt extremely awkward. Finally, Harold said, "Brother Charles will you pray for me?"

"Sure Harold," and I began a prayer with numerous caveats, as I knelt beside him and concluded with "Amen," I looked at Harold, but he did not move. I excused myself and left feeling like a failure.

I went home and prayed and studied. I decided that I had not prayed in faith and that faith was the issue, not oil. I believed that the Lord had set me up, but that He did want to heal Harold, after He dealt with me first.

The next morning, Harold was on the phone again. "Brother Charles, bring your oil and come over; let's pray again."

"Lord, if you don't heal Harold, I'm going to have to do this every day," I thought as I drove to his house.

This time, no small talk. I bent over Harold, poured oil on his forehead, and placed my hand firmly there. "In the name of

Jesus be healed!"

Harold got up on his feet. "Praise God," he said. "I'm healed."

"Me too, Harold."

No, I did not go about healing everyone, but I understood something fresh about faith. Faith acts; men love action and results, especially when it really matters. Health and the ability to work and earn an hourly wage mattered to Harold, to Jesus, and me. Harold later became an evangelist.

God knows how to deal with men—even in their sins. I'm not certain that much of the Church knows how to do that.

Not all men were reached through miracles or healing. Most were reached through lunch, a cup of coffee, or by a good wife who applied her spirituality to pleasing her husband. One thing that I did was to ask the women not to quote me to their husbands, or to use what they learned to make him feel alienated from the Lord or the Church.

One such woman practiced the Scriptures diligently in that regard for 12 years toward a very tough husband. He owned a large company and managed strong men. I'll never forget the day he finally came to a meeting. He was in a wheelchair after a serious stroke and heart attack that had nearly killed him. He was unconscious for days, but God raised him up, and afterward he became a different man, a humble servant of God. His prayers were child-like and sincere.

God made Adam in the very beginning; though he sinned, he must have been a fine specimen of manhood. Then there's Noah, who spent one hundred years building a ship—without power tools. What was he like? And there was Abraham who was having children at more than 100

The percentage of 13-35 year old males who regularly go to church is in steady decline. This fact will cause desperate issues for women and children in the future.

years of age. And then there's Moses, who at 120 years, was of clear vision and still virile. We could list so many more, such as like David the Giant-killer. The point is, God knows how to deal with men—even in their sins. I'm not certain that much of the Church knows how to do that.

The Western Church is declining in its ability to draw men; the Church is increasingly effeminized. That is especially true of the 13-35 year old male. The percentage of that group who regularly go to church is in steady decline—maybe 15-20% of them attend regularly, perhaps less. This fact will cause desperate issues for women and children in the future.

Suppose you have daughters that are faithful believers, whom will they marry? If they marry, how will your grandchildren be raised? Where are the men? They are at sports bars, playing games, hanging out, picking up women, or just giving themselves to making money and buying toys. Should they become fathers, what kind of father would they be?

There's an old saying, "Give a man a fish and he will eat for a day; teach a man to fish and he will sit in a boat and drink beer all day." Maybe Jesus would be out there looking for them. I think that He would.

I recommend David Morrow's book, **Why Men Hate Going to Church**. I also recommend a closer look at Orthodox Judaism and Islam; not as models, but for clues as to why we are failing and why they are succeeding in reaching men, even with a message that is inferior to the Gospel. Jesus demonstrated that the Gospel and its mission will reach men, if practiced as He practiced it.

Our prisons are a testimony to our failure. They are filled with young men, many of whom went to church, but found no appeal there. Maleness in general finds little room in our society beyond sports and military life. Many African-American men are being recruited to Islam.

So where have we gone wrong?

HERE ARE SOME SUGGESTIONS FOR REACHING MEN:

The Church is too much about meetings, **men love action.**

The meetings involve singing—some songs are less than masculine.

The meetings often lack focus and mission, **men love mission.**

Too many church leaders are effeminate—Peter carried a sword.

Jesus drove commerce out of the temple—it's back.

Jesus revealed power—Church is about piety.

Women "fall in love with Jesus"—men will respect, admire, and even trust Him—if the real Jesus is presented.

Church is "sweet"—**men like potency.**

I could go on but you get the picture. That's why men are
best reached outdoors, not indoors. If we fail to understand
men, we will fail to reach them, or any other group that we fail
to understand. More and more men grow up without fathers.
And many who have fathers don't want to become like them—
but they do. I recently spoke to a juvenile judge who said that he
had over 1100 youth on probation. Over 800 were without fathers
at home.

I am not advocating a womanless Church. I am advocating a Church that understands and builds men and women.

I'm not advocating a womanless Church. I am advocating a
Church that understands and builds men and women. I also
highly recommend a book by Mohr and Jessel, **Brain Sex**, that
explores the difference between the male and female brain. I
am advocating churches that understand both men and women.
I'm not sure that better meetings are the answer. I believe that
the answer is in having more masculine mentors who know
how to reach men and teach them how to follow the Jesus of the
Bible. Men must be reached by other men that they can respect:
men who can teach them how to treat a woman and be committed to her well-being; mentors who can teach men how to raise

a family and produce godly children.

My friend Jim McNally has written an excellent book called *Sonship—the Path to Fatherhood*. Because many men never learned to be sons, they never learned to be fathers. This is a proper approach. Jesus came as a Son who revealed the Father. Good mentors have learned to be spiritual sons and can then be spiritual fathers that train spiritual sons, who grow up to become spiritual fathers.

Malachi 4:5-6 gives us the prophetic challenge to reconnect the generations, otherwise we will experience—and are experiencing—a societal curse. In order to reconnect the generations we must reconnect with men. If the Church is to be a family under the Fatherhood of God, then we must rebuild the family model—beginning with men.

CHAPTER ELEVEN
The FLOW *of* MONEY

TO SAY THAT MONEY IS INCONSEQUENTIAL
or a subject to be ignored, is not only gross naiveté, but it
reveals a gross ignorance of Holy Scriptures. From the
resources that built the ark to the jewel-laden gates of heaven,
the Bible speaks about wealth and how it's used. A "vow of
poverty" may be a virtue to someone whose needs are met by
others, but poverty itself is no blessing.

Concepts and methods can be matters of great controversy.
But all of that is abstract until some action is taken. When
things start happening, money starts flowing. Money becomes
the fuel for action and the fuel of opposition. Let's face it: money

empowers. Do you think Ross Perot would have ever been a presidential candidate except for his massive wealth? Would any president ever get elected without vast amounts of money?

This is not about the love of money; it is about the flow of money. Money flows where our life flows. It reveals where our heart is. It may flow toward self-gratification, toward necessities, or toward the needs of others. A lot of it flows toward causes and missions that are of priority importance. But it flows—especially in developed nations.

> **Those who consider money a "side issue" in our stewardship are woefully wrong and do great damage to God's people.**

I will not attempt the massive effort and time to catalogue the biblical references to money, wealth, or resources. I will attempt to state how money is supposed to flow in the Lord's work and how it can fuel the work of the Lord. And I do say that those who considers money a "side issue" in our stewardship are woefully wrong and do great damage to God's people. Giving from a right motive is indeed a blessing that precedes and supersedes receiving. The one who will not give is poorest of all.

I was involved in helping some friends who were being sued, as mentioned in an earlier chapter. The plaintiff's attorney was a high-paid professional with a visceral dislike for Christian faith. He sequestered one of the defendants for a court-ordered deposition, pounding him with questions for hours. The deposition ran 500 pages. The defendant was reduced to tears facing a $44 million lawsuit and an "attack-dog" attorney. Upon reading the deposition, I was outraged at both the plaintiff's attorney and the defendant's attorney that allowed the deposition to go as it did.

The plaintiff's attorney called Jesus "a penniless wanderer" and there was no objection from the defense; nothing could have been farther from the truth. Jesus was neither penniless or a wanderer. His purpose was clear, His direction was clear, He had a treasure, and wore an expensive garment. In addition, He taught about money and how to use it. He spoke of good stewardship and endorsed tithing down to the herbs and

> **Jesus was neither penniliess or a wanderer. His purpose was clear, His direction was clear.**

vegetables in the garden. And He often used money and resources in the stories that he told.

The Scriptures clearly state many issues that pertain to money and examples about money: the Tabernacle and Temple were richly adorned; David gave millions of dollars of his own money to build the Temple; the prophets told that wealth would flow back to Israel; and Malachi rebuked God's people for giving cheap offerings. He called it "robbing God."

> **Jesus commended the widow for giving all she had and condemned the Pharisees for giving to be seen. He taught that faithfulness in money would result in TRUE riches.**

Jesus commended the widow for giving all she had and condemned the Pharisees for giving to be seen. He taught that faithfulness in money would result in true riches. The Early Church sold houses and land to give to the apostles. Paul commended those who gave generously and told Corinth to learn that grace. In Galatians he said, "Let the one who is taught the Word give back to the teacher—all good things." Why? Because good teachings equip for success and the successful person owes the mentor. Both mentor and student are financially blessed through reciprocity.

This is not primarily about tithing, though I believe in it strongly. Some say it is "Old Testament." Indeed, and New Testament too. Abraham tithed to Melchezedek, thus tithing predates the Law. Jacob promised to tithe if God would bless him. That also predated the Law. And of course the Levites received tithes and gave tithes to their superiors. When they got more than they could presently use, they put the tithes into the "store house."

Tithing created a reciprocity. The Levites taught the ways of God; the people prospered and returned tithes to the Levites. When Israel forsook the ways of God, the prosperity ceased and the money stopped flowing; truth and money are "soul-mates"; they work together, but when the people do well and yet serve their own appetite, then money flows to corruption and eventually the economy falters. When the economy supports truth and mercy, it prospers.

Abraham used his wealth to bless others. He was promised that his seed would bless all the families of the earth.

I believe that money should be given to support truth. Truth brings prosperity to the populace. No, the motive is not money; it is a good social condition where resources support the purpose of God, Who in turn blesses the people. The word "bless" means to prosper. I don't fully understand the word blessing, but I know that it makes us better off. It makes us rich and adds no sorrow. Abraham, the wealthy man, was promised that his seed would bless all the families of the earth. Abraham used wealth to bless others. We know from Galatians that Jesus is the Seed of Abraham, who is blessing all nations.

Jesus' mission was to bless all nations with atonement, justification, redemption, reconciliation, and restoration. These are unspeakably wonderful gifts. Wherever they are received, things get better in every way—including economically. Did Jesus love the poor and downtrodden? Of course He did. He became poor so that the poor could be lifted out of poverty and disease. We all know that poverty and disease go together. Why then would Jesus the Healer choose to leave people in poverty?

> **"So you believe there are two kingdoms of God," Hugo asked. "One Kingdom for the U.S. and another for Latin America?" "No," I replied. "Then giving works for us, just as it does for you."He smiled as he said it.**

Our daughter works among the poor in Latin America. One of the first things she noticed was the poverty, and that they had not been taught how to give. Both religion and socialism had taught so many of them to be dependent on someone else. "They are too poor to give," some would say. But my friend Hugo Zelaya, an apostle among his own people in Costa Rica taught people to give, even in their poverty (see 2 Corinthians 8:1-7). They have been blessed by God in doing so, and they are prospering.

When I speak to Brother Zelaya's people, they give me generous offerings. At first I was reluctant to receive it because I was financially better off than most of them. "So, you believe that there are two kingdoms of God," Hugo asked. "One Kingdom for the U.S. and another for Latin America?" "No," I replied. "Then giving works for us, just as it does for you." He smiled as he said it. But I knew that my refusal to accept the offering was a "put down;" I was patronizing my Latin brothers and sisters in Christ.

When I was very young Dad and Mom taught me to tithe. "Save some, spend some, give some," Dad would say, "But the first tenth belongs to God."

In 1948, at age eleven, I got a job in a grocery store and my boss promised three dollars for working all day Saturday. At the close of the day, he handed me a check for two dollars and forty cents. "What about the other sixty cents?" I asked.

"Sixty cents for social security and income tax," he broke the news; I only had two dollars and forty cents.

Being a tither, I had to figure out, "Do I tithe the net or the gross?"

So, I asked Dad that serious question; it was six cents difference. I could buy a popsicle for six cents. I waited for Dad's answer. He looked at me for a moment then said, "Do what's in your heart." I still had a problem, not wanting God to know what was really in my heart. I gave the entire thirty cents.

Since then, I discovered the principle, "faithful in a little, given much" (see Luke 16:10-12).

> **God is a giver, and the purpose of God is to make us gracious and generous. It is the goodness of God that leads people to repent. So, our generosity opens people to the Gospel.**

Generosity is giving more than necessary. Proverbs 11:23-24 tells us that the generous person will "be made fat" or have plenty. The one that scatters abroad will himself receive back. Generosity is a godly quality. God is the God of abundance—more than we can imagine. God is a giver, and the purpose of God is to make us gracious and generous. It is the goodness of God that leads people to repent. So, our generosity opens people to the Gospel.

When Hurricane Katrina hit the Gulf Coast in August 2005, our supporters helped us to give $300,000 to the victims. Time after time, we saw a positive spiritual effect of giving. The U.S. response to the Asian tsunami and the earthquake relief in Pakistan opened people in those areas to our nation and the Gospel. Don't tell them that money is unimportant.

If I mentored someone who failed to tithe and be generous,

I would think myself a failure in that case. Yet many leaders fail to take it personally when their constituents give meagerly. I know of large churches that accept small giving. They think that they are doing those people a favor by not mentioning giving. But they are failing their people in the area of money.

Sam Jones, the great Methodist Evangelist, was passing a bar in a rundown area during prohibition. A bartender, thinking to have some fun with the preacher, ran out and offered Jones twenty dollars—a lot of money then. Jones took the twenty.

"Don't eat at Howard Johnson's and pay at Holiday Inn." —Derek Prince

"But Reverend, you know that's liquor money!" the owner protested.

"Yes sir, and it's served the devil long enough," Jones smiled.

If money is to serve the Lord's work, where do we send it? Great question. My friend Derek Prince used to say, "You don't eat at Howard Johnson's and pay at Holiday Inn." You pay where you eat.

What about the store house? The store house is where the minister takes it for future use. And the store house is where help can be gotten in the time of need. Money should flow to where life is received. Hopefully, that will be the local church. But, I believe we give to the ministry of life and the Word of God. If your church is not ministering life and the Word of God, maybe you should go and give elsewhere or at least challenge the church to minister life.

Of course charity is a different matter. Charity is giving above the tithe based on the needs of others (see Matthew 25:31-46). Tithe and charity should never be confused. Generosity is still

> **"Money talks; it usually says goodbye." Money will flow, and if it flows toward consumption, it corrupts. If it flows to the needy, the Lord keeps a record.**

another matter. I always tip those who serve me in restaurants and do so at least a fifteen percent rate. My sophomore year in college, I worked for tips. Generosity is a virtue—believe me.

Someone said, "Money talks; it usually says goodbye." Money will flow, and if it flows toward consumption, it corrupts. If it flows to the needy, the Lord keeps a record. If it flows to the truth, the blessings of truth follow. If it flows to the sources of ministry, more ministries are fueled. Money is the measure of how society values service, time, and energy. The money that we give is a measure of our life priorities and compassion. It is always an accurate one.

The new ecclesiology, like the old one, will be fueled with money. As people look for a more direct relationship to the results of their giving, they will look for a more direct relationship with their pastors, mentors, and leaders. That is where the money will—and should—flow. Where life and blessing are found, money will be found there. But woe to the

> **Woe to the leader who serves for the love of money. Woe to the leader who does not himself tithe and give generously. He or she will be found out in due course and the reaping will be sorrowful.**

leader who serves for the love of money. Woe to the leader who does not himself tithe and give generously. He or she will be found out in due course. And then reaping will be sorrowful.

Sowers will be reapers—whatever they sow. Those that sow precious seed even in tears, will return rejoicing bringing the harvest with them (see Psalm 126).

CHAPTER TWELVE

The *Mystery*
Of FELLOWSHIP

∎

THE APOSTLE PAUL SAYS THAT WE ARE THE
fellowship of the mystery (see Ephesians 3:9). Of traditional
church meetings, my friend Bob Mumford used to say, "You
cannot fellowship the back of someone's head." And that is the
dilemma of traditional church structure. Fellowship is shared
life; it happens on a personal level, in small groups, before or
after the meeting. Women love fellowshipping together. Once
talking together, it is hard to pull them apart. "Come on Honey,
it is time to go home." "Okay, Sweetheart." Fifteen minutes go
by, "Okay, Dear, I'm leaving."

Guys enjoy it too. They will sit over a drink for hours swapping stories and telling of exploits, when the ladies are not around. Something mysterious is going on. Each person has plugged into something that is recharging their battery. They are giving, receiving, and sharing life. We know that this mystery exists, but we fail to understand it.

We are made for fellowship. Adam was made for God, but he needed Eve. Of course, "hanging out" was something the devil tried in the Garden also.

We are made for fellowship. Adam was made for God, but he needed Eve. Of course "hanging out" was something the devil tried in the Garden also.

People go to church to find fellowship but often don't. They wind up going to some place "where everybody knows your name."

Jesus understood fellowship. Soon after beginning His ministry, He began to look up guys near where He grew up. He understood them and invested most of His time with them. They were all together so much that eventually they came to be like Him. They came to really know who He was as they talked and walked together.

One day, He asked them, "Who do you say that I am?" Peter said, "You are the Christ, the Son of the Living God." He said, "You are blessed Peter, my Father in heaven showed you that." Many times they heard stories given to the multitude, or some group of religious leaders, that concealed mysteries, but Jesus said that the mysteries were only for them. The deep truths get shared with friends.

Then one day He said, "When two or three of you gather together in My name, I'll be there with you."

> ## Suddenly, in the distance a storm was brewing. Storms come up fast on the Gulf of Mexico, and we did not want to try to beat it back to the harbor. "Why don't we rebuke it like Jesus did?" someone suggested.

A beautiful day in 1973 was like that for me and a few friends. We were sailing on the Gulf of Mexico in a schooner—a two-masted rig that flew five sails and was over fifty feet in length. Nothing was heard but the sound of the breeze moving through the sails and the waters splashing along the side of the boat.

Several of us sat in the spacious aft cockpit occasionally talking about the Lord, and the deep sense that it was a special season of change. Suddenly, in the distance, a storm was brewing. Storms come up fast on the Gulf of Mexico, and we did not want to try to beat it back to the harbor.

"Why don't we rebuke it like Jesus did?" someone suggested. We decided to do just that; His presence was with us. We stood up in the cockpit, "We rebuke you, storm, in the name of Jesus! Go away and dissipate!"

In a few moments we could see the storm turn and go away. We returned to fellowship, but with a strange awareness of His presence. Were we being called to chase storms? No, we were called to fellowship. And the Lord was there.

> **"What is more like what Jesus did with his disciples...what we are doing today, or what we will do tomorrow at church?" Then I asked, "What is more like the Pharisees did?" There was a nervous laugh.**

We were quiet for a while, then I asked, "What is more like what Jesus did with His disciples... what we are doing today, or what we will do tomorrow at church?" Then I asked, "What is more like the Pharisees did?" There was a nervous laugh; we all regularly went to church. Then it was quiet for a while—just the wind and the water.

All of these men were then—or would become—pastors. But the Lord was pointing out something vital to the new ecclesiology—it's about fellowship around Jesus.

Too often we are caught up in the gift of... or ministry of... or the office of... and have little place for just pure fellowship, We are too busy solving problems; He is calling us back to fellowship. Psalm 133 says that where brothers dwell together in unity, it's like the oil that flowed down Aaron's beard, all the way to the bottom of his robe. It's like the dew on Mt. Herman that flows southward and brings a river to Zion. There, God commands a blessing. Something mysterious and beneficial happens in social and spiritual harmony.

Harmony is a beautiful and pleasant sound. In college, I was privileged to sing in the choir of a local church. We performed "The Messiah." It was one of my favorite experiences of youth. We rehearsed for many, many hours. On one occasion when we did the dress rehearsal, it was unusually well done. A grand piano was on stage and as we concluded the "Hallelujah Chorus," in the silence the strings of the piano began to vibrate and continued for a few moments. It was eerily beautiful.

The director finally

> **The piano began to vibrate. It was eerily beautiful. The director finally spoke, "Overtones," he said. "The piano was saying, 'amen,' and you are all on key." I had never heard that before or since.**

spoke, "Overtones," he said. "The piano was saying, 'amen,' and you are all on key." I had never heard that before—or since.

When we are all together, in harmony, heaven says, "Amen." Fellowship is "tuning up" for the heavenly choir.

The first vision that I ever had was shortly after being baptized in the Holy Spirit. I saw a great choir, the size of half of a football stadium. They were singing a new song—in the Holy Spirit. I couldn't make out the words, but the sound enthralled me. They were not basses, altos, tenors, and sopranos—each person sang a different part. The volume weaved in and out of the vast choir as it had a corporate pulsating vibrato. It sounded like a great harp touched by the fingers of God. Then in the center and below the choir, I saw the back of Jesus who directed them. I heard three things: "I made their voices, each one unique. I wrote the music; each person has a purpose. And, I'll direct them myself." I took the last sentence as a warning.

> "I made their voices, each one unique. I wrote the music; each person has a purpose. And I'll direct them myself."

Harmony, what a mystery; God loves it. Discord what a misery; God hates it. Wherever there's harmony among humans—He's bound to be there. The notes linger in the air, and people hear from afar and are drawn to it. But discord? They run from it.

One work horse can pull 9,000 pounds of dead weight. Two can pull 27,000.

One work horse can pull nine thousand pounds of dead weight. Two should pull eighteen thousand pounds of dead weight. But no, they pull twenty-seven thousand pounds of dead weight. Where two horses are yoked together—a "third one" pulls with them, another mystery of fellowship. I'm sure some scientist can tell me why these things are true. But no one seems to bring us together—except Christ.

Fellowship—God loves it and Satan hates it. Satan hated it in heaven, in the Garden, in the family, in Israel, in church, in nations, and among nations. Why? He fears its power. His pride caused him to create discord in heaven, but God cast him out. He created discord between Adam and Eve, Adam and God, Cain and Abel, society and God, and on and on.

How is the enemy so successful? He uses our own appetites against us. He urges us to serve ourselves, suspect others, and return acts in kind. He will do anything including lying and murdering to create chaos—and he rules there. Thank God, the accuser of the brethren "has been cast down!" He roams the earth, but does not reign in heaven. I have seen churches accept the "accuser of the brethren" into their membership. But he is not welcomed in heaven.

I saw it one night when I was five years old. I saw it again years later when I visited a church on Wednesday night, not knowing that it would be a "business meeting." I saw it again as the church that I pastored became inflamed with controversy and people who had loved one another spoke terribly to each other—as they discussed "The Holy Spirit."

> **I have seen churches accept the "accuser of the brethren" into their membership. But he is not welcomed in heaven.**

I saw it in pastors conferences and in denominational meetings. I heard arguments over the gifts. While someone said in a loud voice, "The greatest gift is love!" Another responded "If love is the greatest gift... where is it?"

I learned in all of this that religion, education, politics, or philosophy do not have ability to prevent discord. It's the number one human contact sport. Of course the ultimate expression of discord is when people really get killed.

As our church was spiraling into controversy over speaking in tongues, I announced that I would speak on "Tongues of Fire." Even on Sunday night, the church was full as people waited for a message that they thought it would be on

"UNKNOWN TONGUES." The "telephone committee" had been busy. Instead, I preached from James 3:5-6—"Tongues Set on Fire of Hell"—gossip. I don't know if it helped, but I felt good doing it.

This reminds me of a story my friend Glen Roachelle told me: "A man's pickup truck broke down in front of a bar in a small town. He pushed it to the curb and left it in the front of the bar—all night. The village gossip heard that his truck was there all night and began a rumor that the man was a drunk and living a life of sin. He heard the rumor and after getting his truck fixed, he parked it in front of her house—all night."

We all have too many fears. What we do not understand, we fear, and what we fear, we fight. God's love casts out fear, brings security, and allows us into fellowship with the Father,

> **There has been a loss of fellowship among Christians, and as a result, a great loss of spiritual power among us and through us. Carnal thinking has produced unending division and animosity. But something fresh is happening—RECONCILIATION.**

the Son, and one another. We can know and be known among those God puts in our life. (Of course the "village gossip" should not be invited to personal sharing.) Fellowship will ultimately teach us whom we can trust. But in it all we must trust God. He knows us best and loves us most.

There has been a loss of fellowship among Christians, and as a result, a great loss of spiritual power among us and through us. Carnal thinking has produced unending division, and animosity. But something fresh is happening—reconciliation. Perhaps having been processed through our own failure, and humbled at our own cross, we can find each other again; this time not in idealism, but in grace. Perhaps the choir will sing again and the strings will say "Amen."

WHATEVER the "New Church Structure" may be, it may be years before most of the larger Church will embrace it. Some never will. All of us are challenged to do more than champion one particular form. We are challenged to love one another. Utopianism and triumphalism are contrary to the Spirit of Christ. Fellowship with Him requires fellowship with each other.

> **One person suggested to Mom, "Maybe you didn't move far enough away." Mom cried.**

Traditional structures may be challenged in the area of spiritual community and small groups, but then small groups are unlikely to perform Handel's "Messiah." We need both the corporate and the personal emphasis.

I have been blessed by both traditional and emerging forms. But I cherish the relationships that have endured for many years due to the way I have experienced church, without attacking other models. I enjoy my enduring spiritual family and the generations that are being produced.

I saw Mom and Dad lose that after thirty-five years at one church. The church got a new pastor. He lasted one year. Dad had visited the hospital, but the new guy just "sent cards". Dad and Mom moved and wouldn't go back, in order to make room for the new pastor, and the other pastors that followed. That was the ethical way to do it, so that is what they did.

One person suggested to Mom, after they retired, "Maybe you didn't move far enough away." Mom cried. But that is church. Old pastors are used up, have little money, and a young naïve pastor stands in his pulpit—maybe in the building the old guy built. But the new pastor may lack understanding about spiritual family.

Fortunately, the same parents that had given me family at birth were able to be part of our family and spiritual family for twenty more years and give to us the "gold and silver that they possessed" through vibrant ministry and sharing life together.

Am I angry about that? No, I love those people whom my Dad served for thirty-five years. They only did what churches do—and as Dad said, "I taught them."

What I do pray is, that sometime in God's time, our journey will take us back to apostolic faith operating through apostolic channels of grace. I pray for structures that release the Gospel in the power of God, structures that are alive, personal and flexible, and structures that allow God's people to be a family, not just an audience. It is happening some places in the world. May it happen where you are.

Bob Mumford was a pioneer in the Charismatic movement. In the late 1960s through the early 1980s, he and I often ministered together. Tragically, in 1985, we separated. For 20 years, he and I remained apart. Then, in 2006, we reconciled and ministered together again. We both publicly apologized for our contribution to the division. It brought indescribable joy to us and those who loved us. It also motivated others to seek reconciliation.

Is the Church looking at a lesson of restored fellowship and power? I pray so. It is time to look beyond conflict, give grace and forgiveness to one another, and work together to solve our mutual challenges. I recommend Ken Sumrall's book *Forgive and Move On*. After all, it is the will of God.

If we can seek humility, embrace the Cross, and follow the Holy Spirit, we will see the knowledge of the glory of the Lord cover the earth as the waters cover the sea. We will also see the flow of God's grace, increased resources, and a great wave of evangelism.

So, if you are doing your service as unto the Lord, and you love His Church, then here's to your success!

5642733R0

Made in the USA
Charleston, SC
15 July 2010